Who's Writing This?

Who's Writing This?

Notations on
the Authorial I
with Self-Portraits

Edited by
Daniel Halpern

THE ECCO PRESS

THE ECCO PRESS
100 West Broad Street
Hopewell, New Jersey 08525
Published simultaneously in Canada by
Penguin Books Canada Ltd., Ontario
Printed in the United States of America
Designed by Richard Oriolo
FIRST EDITION

Library of Congress Cataloging-in-Publication Data

Who's writing this? : notations on the authorial I with self-
portraits / edited by Daniel Halpern.
p.   cm.
1. Authorship.   2. Self in literature.   3. Point of view
(Literature)   4. First person narrative.   5. Persona (Literature)
I. Halpern, Daniel, 1945–
PN145.W45   1994
801'.92—dc20 94-17421
ISBN 0-88001-377-X

The text of this book is set in ITC Berkeley Old Style

As I ebbed with the ocean of life,
As I wended the shores I know,
As I walked where the sea-ripples wash you, Paumanok,
Where they rustle up, hoarse and sibilant,
Where the fierce old mother endlessly cries for her
    castaways,
I, musing, late in the autumn day, gazing off southward,
Alone, held by the eternal self of me that threatens to get the
    better of me, and stifle me,
Was seized by the spirit that trails in the lines underfoot,
In the rim, the sediment, that stands for all the water and all
    the land of the globe.

Fascinated, my eyes, reverting from the south, dropped, to
    follow those slender windrows,
Chaff, straw, splinters of wood, weeds, and the sea-gluten,
Scum, scales from shining rocks, leaves of salt-lettuce, left by
    the tide,
Miles walking, the sound of breaking waves the other side
    of me,
Paumanok, there and then, as I thought the old thought of
    likenesses,
These you presented to me, you fish-shaped island,
As I wended the shores I know,
As I walked with that eternal self of me, seeking types.

—WALT WHITMAN

Contents

Daniel Halpern

Why Who?—A Preface

*W*ho *is* doing the writing? Given the opportunity to spoof and play, the fifty-six writers included in *Who's Writing This? Notations on the Authorial I with Self-Portraits* have addressed a notion of what seems to happen at the moment of composition, using as prototype the signature Borges mini-essay, "Borges and I." They have articulated, in terms of *relationship*, that atmosphere that produces, in W. H. Auden's phrase, "verbal objects." We meet, via *namesake, pseudonym, nom de plum, doppelganger, twin, surrogate, falsifier, impersonator* (close relations all)—a variety of *types*, or, in some cases, *archetypes*—the writers we always thought were singular entities, whose purpose was the solitary act of committing the imagination to immortality. Borges writes, "It is to my other self, to Borges, that things happen." What's created here is an imaginary dichotomy, the fictional persona "behind the scenes," the *he* and *she* who lift and twist the strings, simultaneously identifying with the puppet—an alter (altered?) ego, an *I* not necessarily *I*, nor *me*, as it were.

These pieces have been assembled to introduce an internalized persona—and the pursuant lifelong comrade, the significant other—capable of expressing the honest lie, the fictive truth. Throughout, we discern, albeit between the lines, a certain nervousness, in some cases embarrassed jubilation. Of course, the fallacy is modesty, the implied (and good-natured!) Dickensian 'umble man, the unstated green room of the ego: Someone else is writing this? Someone writing this in my name? Well, the fiction throughout the essays is not so much in the writing as in the attribution. The uninitiated might be led to venture forth an innocent query of their own: "But is no one of *you* capable of writing this?"

Who's Writing This?

Jorge Luis Borges

Translated from the Spanish by Alastair Reid

Borges and I

I t is to my other self, to Borges, that things happen. I walk about Buenos Aires and I pause, almost mechanically, to contemplate the arch of an entry or the portal of a church; news of Borges comes to me in the mail, and I see his name on a short list of professors or in a biographical dictionary. I am fond of hourglasses, maps, eighteenth-century typography, the etymology of words, the tang of coffee, and the prose of Stevenson; the other one shares these enthusiasms, but in a rather vain, theatrical way. It would be an exaggeration to call our relationship hostile. I live, I agree to go on living, so that Borges may fashion his literature; that literature justifies me. I do not mind admitting that he has managed to write a few worthwhile pages, but these pages cannot save me, perhaps because good writing belongs to nobody, not even to my other, but rather to language itself, to the tradition. Beyond that, I am doomed to oblivion, utterly doomed, and no more than certain flashes of my existence can survive in the work of my other. Little by little I am surrendering everything to him, although I am well aware of his perverse habit of falsifying and exaggerating. Spinoza understood that everything wishes to continue in its own being: A stone wishes to be a stone, eternally, a tiger a tiger. I must go on in

Borges, not in myself (if I am anyone at all). But I recognize myself much less in the books he writes than in many others or in the clumsy plucking of a guitar. Years ago I tried to cut free from him and I went from myths of suburban life to games with time and infinity; but those games belong to Borges now and I will have to come up with something else. And so my life leaks away and I lose everything, and everything passes into oblivion, or to my other.

I cannot tell which one of us is writing this page.

Diane Ackerman

Diane Ackerman and I

"*I* am no longer responsible for any acts committed by my previous selves." That's one motto, Ackerman confided to me, by which she wished she could live. Selves will accumulate when one isn't looking, and they don't always act wisely or well. This was not what she had expected when she was little, growing up in the Midwest, where the snows were shoulder high, piles of leaves could be dived into, and her life shone before her as a clear trajectory. It was the fairy tale she had been told to expect: A Knight in Shining Armor would appear suddenly to guide her and heal her life; then she would produce two children, buy a dog, work at a pleasant job, and live forever in an oasis of calm. A boarder in her house, I became her lifelong confidante. I sometimes gossiped with her about the Bohemian lives of artists; but we never dreamed that she would grow up to live such a life herself.

It was only in her middle years that she began to notice how her selves had been forming layer upon layer, translucent like skin; and, like skin, they were evolving a certain identifiable "fingerprint"—a weather system of highs and lows, loops and whirls. Yes, she revealed one day, as she pulled back the thick rind on an orange, feeling the zest spray over her cheeks and nose, her caravan of selves probably began when she was little, inventing mental adventures in which she starred. Her daily life was unbearable. Had it been mine, I would have run away, but she fled mentally along the Silk Road of the imagination.

One continuing fantasy was that she was not human, but rather an extraterrestrial, part of a group of itinerant artists who traveled throughout the universe. On their planet, art was deeply revered and prized, and, above all, they relished discovering the arts of various life forms, because it revealed so much about heart and needs, values, and yearnings. Each itinerant artist was born into the civilization of a planet and grew up soul-drenchingly creative, remembering nothing of the planet of origin.

Her job was to feel and so she *felt,* penetratingly, exhaltingly, agonizingly. She peered for long hours into the hidden recesses of things. She trotted after thoughts to see where they led. And, in time, she created a beautiful sampler of the range of human feeling and experience. Then, towards what she naturally imagined to be the end of her life, she one day heard a voice saying to her: "Come to the window. The night air is sweet. . . . "

Decoyed from her doings by the simple beauty of the evening, she went to the window, inhaled the scent of jasmine drifting in, and was suddenly amazed to see an alien standing there. All at once her mission became clear to her; she knew her work was done on Earth, that her destiny was to rest a while on the small city-state of the mothership, and then be born on a new planet, into another species, to undergo extremes of feeling, and create art from that amalgam of privilege and ordeal. Learning she was not human shocked and saddened her, and she begged to be allowed to remain human. The separation was grueling. Humans were among the most emotional and volatile of all the planetarians in the universe, but human was what she knew and loved and she could not bear the thought of leaving, leaving with so much still unexplored and unvoiced. "It is enough," she was assured. "There are other worlds to explore, other beings to become." And so she went with him to the spaceship just beyond Earth's orbit, and rejoined her troupe of artists, some of whom like her were between lives. That otherworldly dream haunted her early years and adolescence, and she half expected that one day she really would be summoned to the hidden part of her destiny with a whisper: "Come to the window. The night air is sweet. . . . "

Older, what she craved was to be ten or twelve selves, each passionately committed to a different field—a dancer, a carpenter, a composer, an astronaut, a miner, etc. Some would be male, some female, and all of their sensations would feed back to one central source. Surely then she would begin to understand the huge spill of life, if she could perceive it from different view points, through simultaneous lives. Once I accused her of being fickle, but she answered simply "not fickle, just curious." She had been writing since she was little. If she couldn't actually live simultaneous lives, perhaps she could do so serially—by giving herself passionately, blood and bones, to what she wrote about, by *becoming* her subjects.

Her most recent self lives in a small town of trees, waterfalls and flowers, where most people know or at least recognize one another, and many of their stories converge. From time to time, she travels to distant places in pursuit of the marvelous. But, after all, the marvelous is a populous species; it thrives everywhere, even in yards and ditches. So she always returns home. There, through the many windows of a house in the woods, she watches the doings of the deer, squirrels, birds, and metamorphosing seasons. She thinks a lot about the pageant of being human—what it senses, loves, suffers, thrills like—while working silently in a small room, filling blank sheets of paper. It is a solitary mania. But there are times when, all alone, she could be arrested for unlawful assembly.

Edward Albee

I look at myself in the mirror and see I am not looking back at myself. I am seeing him. I am seeing him looking at me, looking through me to himself, to see the reflection in his eyes of himself looking at himself through me. I vanish then, for it is not true we all see what we wish.

I look at him in the mirror and see he is not looking back at me. He is looking at himself. He is seeing through me to himself. I vanish once again.

I turn my back to the mirror, and I sense he has done so, too. I cannot be certain, but I think he has. I wonder if he is waiting for me to turn. I wonder if I turn who's eyes will meet who's eyes, who will be looking through who's eyes to whom. I dare not turn, for I know I will vanish.

Max Apple

Borges and I [10]

To: My dear Borges dead and still teasing

From: All of us

Re: One plus one

*B*orges and Borges holding words down the page, how quaint. The dreamy dreamer dreams, the bundle of flesh drives the car, buys groceries, talks to the proofreader. It's downright classical, worthy of a rhymed couplet, a flourish of trumpets, a minuet, a powdered wig, a mill, a steam engine, . . . but who are we kidding, Borges?

There haven't been two since before there was one. Let's start with the divided self, then up the numbers—say about 10^{10} times. Let's add in all those sperm that didn't make it but are still represented by counsel, then every solid atom, the sticky community of molecules, the fateful DNA twisted like a challah. Maybe for you metaphorists all that equals a one, but for us in the pits of the imagination, there's no ones, only democracy and statistics. Down here the unspoken, the forgotten, the un-thought, the nonexistent, we're the ones who do the speed-of-light drudgery. We're like slaves captured to row those Roman triremes. We're down below heaving, sweating, as forgotten as old pay stubs. While you watch the stately sentence sail across the page as if there really was a wind, we're squirting life blood to make it to the period.

Sure we envy the real, especially memories, those hot shots who sit up top in the reserved section with security guards and makeup crews. They strut around like movie stars all full of themselves just because they happen to have happened. What didn't happen is our business. An example: Take Carol Kross, a girl the writer never knew in seventh grade. She's been leaning against a locker waiting since 1953. Her bobby sox are rolled to her ankle. She's wearing a little blue sweater and a circle pin and a padded bra. She's standing on one foot, the bottom of her saddle shoe against a locker.

No doubt, she fell in love. Maybe he died in Vietnam, then she remarried a long-distance trucker, and now she's a perky grandma who doesn't even remember her ovaries, but we've still got her at the locker, waiting. Give her a chance, put her on the page and she might become Anna Karenina, Moll Flanders, who knows? She still hopes. Since '53 she's been waving at every passing syllable, yoo-hooing the paragraphs. Sure, it takes time and energy to keep her ready, but that's the coin of our realm. Down here every sneeze is a typhoon and there's an ice age between heartbeats.

When that little pisher Apple finally gets down to work, when he rubs his beard, to us it's an air raid. He puts in his earplugs and looks out the window, . . . nothing happens; to us it's like a submarine diving. By the time he cranks out a little sentence, millions of us have drowned, and then he scratches it out. With our last breath we whisper, "Give us numbers, give us Stephen King, Joyce Carol Oates, Shakespeare, the O.E.D."

We're not ones, we're galaxies, sinking sentence by sentence beneath reason and grammar and plot, but we've got the real thing, the true story of how each word plops into place. We're as steady as the temperature of the universe. Tune us in between the period and the capital letter, then sit back and listen for the hum. We've been waiting for you.

Margaret Atwood

Me, She, and It

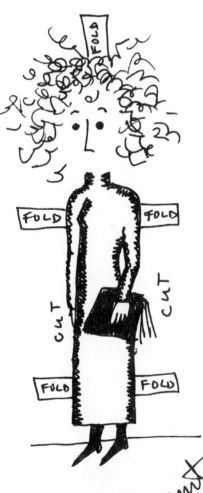

*W*hy do authors wish to pretend they don't exist? It's a way of skinning out, of avoiding truth and consequences. They'd like to deny the crime, although their fingerprints are all over the martini glasses, not to mention the hacksaw blade and the victim's neck. Amnesia, they plead. Epilepsy. Sugar overdose. Demonic possession. How convenient to have an authorial twin, living in your body, looking out through your eyes, pushing pen down on paper or key down on keyboard, while you do what? File your nails?

It was me, I confess it. Or, to be more authorial: It was I.

But please note: The *was* is crucial. By the time you read these words, the *I* that wrote them will have forgotten what *it* was, though the *it* lingers on, haunting the paper, unheard until you happen across it and your energy field activates it, and a voice plays eerily in your head, like a long-forgotten gramophone. At the same time a miasmic image rises like a spirit from a bog. Wavering, indistinct, part fear, part wish-fulfillment, she is me as you conceive me. You even supply the costumes: gauzy Madonna whites, black leather and whips, brisk little suits, they are all your doing. I myself own none of these clothes. A projection, a mass hallucination, a neurological disorder—call her what you will, but don't confuse her with me. She had nothing to do with writing this text, this *it*, which was performed by me, and by me alone, with a blue Express ballpoint pen on a Hilary lined notepad—I supply the brand names to convince you—on a boat crossing Lake Erie, this sixth of September, 1993.

A date which, even as I set it down, assumes the slipperiness, the liquid shine, the alluring phosphorescence of the most devious and lie-inspired fiction. How can you believe it? How can you believe anything I say? That's always the problem, though it's never hers. She's the one you find plausible, she's the one who takes you in, because she is your creature.

But I am not.

Russell Banks

R(&I)

RB

*A*t the first sitting, he leans forward in his chair and looks warily at me, but he cannot say what he is wary of. I write this as a friend, I tell him, and assure him that the people I portray always look handsome, distinguished, and intelligent.

Stiffened and slightly uncomfortable inside his body, he feels at first that nothing is happening. It is like sitting in a dentist's chair having his jaw X-rayed. Then, instead of feeling, as with an X ray, that his body has been invisibly penetrated, he observes that, worse, something is being *removed* from his body, something like its outermost layer of skin, one that he did not realize could be separated from the others.

It is not a layer of his skin that I am removing, however; it is merely the light that is reflected off the surface of his body. Nevertheless, he believes that it is his. He has always owned that light; he needs it to surround the darkness; he wants to keep it.

He fears that somehow he is being slightly diminished by the experience. It occurs to him that if he allows it to continue, if he goes on sitting for me over and over again, year after year, he will not merely become invisible, he will literally disappear—he will cease to exist. The skin of light that surrounds his body will be removed, layer by layer, all the way in to the center, shrinking the darkness inside as it goes, until it is the size of a doll's darkness, then that of the darkness inside an olive, a drop of red wine, a period at the end of a sentence.

When the sitting is over and he is able to speak, he quickly declares his name, *Russell,* as if it were a complete sentence, as if he were using it to claim his table at a restaurant, and his anxiety flies away, like a dream on waking. I cease writing and put down my pen. He feels as if nothing has happened. Surely he imagined it, the loss, the theft, the subatomic pilferage. Perhaps it was a dream of being photographed and was merely symbolic.

Sometime later, he finds himself seated before me in a chair again, and he recalls of the dream of being photographed only the terrible anticipation of loss that it gave him, and without knowing exactly why, grows wary all over again. But the darkness inside his body is smaller now than it was before, and he is not as afraid of losing it as he was the first time.

Perhaps he will smile and look straight into my eyes, and now when I put down my pen, he will not be able to say my name or will remember only its initial letter.

Frank Bidart

Borges and I

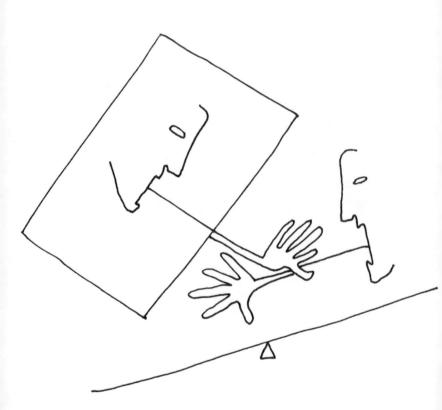

*W*e fill pre-existing forms and when we fill them we change them and are changed.

The desolating landscape in Borges' "Borges and I"—in which the voice of "I" tells us that its other self, Borges, is the self who makes literature, who in the process of making literature falsifies and exaggerates, while the self that is speaking to us now must go on living so that Borges may continue to fashion literature—is seductive and even oddly comforting, but, I think, false.

The voice of this "I" asserts a disparity between its essential self and its worldly second self, the self who seeks embodiment through making things, through work, who in making takes on something false, inessential, inauthentic.

The voice of this "I" tells us that Spinoza understood that everything wishes to continue in its own being, a stone wishes to be a stone eternally, that all "I" wishes is to remain unchanged, itself.

With its lonely emblematic title, "Borges and I" seems to be offered as a paradigm for the life of consciousness, the life of knowing and making, the life of the writer.

The notion that Frank has a self that has remained the same and that knows what it would be if its writing self did not exist—like all assertions about the systems that hold sway beneath the moon, the opposite of this seems to me to be true, as true.

When Borges' "I" confesses that Borges falsifies and exaggerates it seems to do so to cast aside falsity and exaggeration, to attain an entire candor unobtainable by Borges.

This "I" therefore allows us to enter an inaccessible magic space, a hitherto inarticulate space of intimacy and honesty earlier denied us, where voice, for the first time, has replaced silence.

—Sweet fiction, in which bravado and despair beckon from a cold panache, in which the protected essential self suffers flashes of its existence to be immortalized by a writing self that is incapable of performing its actions without mixing our essence with what is false.

Frank had the illusion, when he talked to himself in the cliches he used when he talked to himself, that when he made his poems he was changed in making them, that arriving at the order the poem suddenly arrived at out of the chaos of the materials the poem let enter itself out of the chaos of life, consciousness then, only then, could know itself, Sherlock Holmes was somebody or something before cracking its first case but not Sherlock Holmes, act is the cracked mirror not only of motive but self, *no other way,* tiny mirror that fails to focus in small the whole of the great room.

But Frank had the illusion that his poems also had cruelly replaced his past, that finally they were all he knew of it though he knew they were not, everything else was shards refusing to make a pattern and in any case he had written about his mother and father until the poems saw as much as he saw and saw more and he only saw what he saw in the act of making them.

He had never had a self that wished to continue in its own being, survival meant ceasing to be what its being was.

Frank had the illusion that though the universe of one of his poems seemed so close to what seemed his own universe at the second of writing it that he wasn't sure how they differed even though the paraphernalia often differed, after he had written it its universe was never exactly his universe, and so, soon, it disgusted him a little, the mirror was dirty and cracked.

Secretly he was glad it was dirty and cracked, because after he had made a big order, a book, only when he had come to despise it a little, only after he had at last given up the illusion that this was what was, only then could he write more.

He felt terror at the prospect of becoming again the person who could find or see or make no mirror, for even Olivier, trying to trap the beast who had killed his father, when he suavely told Frank as Frank listened to the phonograph long afternoons lying on the bed as a kid, when Olivier told him what art must be, even Olivier insisted that art is a mirror held up by an artist who himself needs to see something, held up before a nature that recoils before it.

We fill pre-existing forms and when we fill them we change them and are changed.

Everything in art is a formal question, so he tried to do it in prose with much blank white space.

Roy Blount Jr.

Blount, Borges, and I*

*Alphabetically

*A*m I Borges? Don't ask me. For three reasons.

The first, that *I* and *me* are textual conventions—and while it may be no worse than premodern to assume that *I* and *me* are in cahoots, it flouts grammar to expect *me* to identify *I*. *Me* is objective, and cannot get anything done.

The second, that Borges can be deceiving.

The third, if I *am* Borges, I may be beyond all asking by the time you read this statement, which I am dictating after being absolutely blown away by the 1986 Penguin edition of Blount's incredible collection of fiction and nonfiction, *Not Exactly What I Had in Mind,* which I intend to translate into Spanish if it's the last thing I do, and whose influence, I dare say, my own work will henceforth reflect.

At this point you (you know who you are) may be asking: If this endorsement *is* by Borges, why has Blount not exploited it? Assuming he will not have done so. (He certainly has my permission.)

One, maybe he thought it would be in questionable taste.

Two, maybe he thought no one would believe it.

Three, maybe the transcript fell through the cracks, as they say, and only recently turned up.

Four, maybe the person to whom I am dictating (ahem) is jealous of the impact Blount has had on me.

Five, maybe Blount will think it best to submit this to some estimable literary magazine under his own name. That would be my suggestion. But you know me.

—J.L.B.
4/1/86

Sadly, as we all know, Borges did not live to carry out the intentions voiced above. The fifth Borgesian *maybe,* however, has proved uncannily prophetic. Arguably, in fact, all five apply:

- Even now (although a blurb from Borges would surely inspire Penguin to rush *Not Exactly* into a huge new printing), Blount may well question the tastefulness of quoting even such an excerpt as "Incredible—Jorge Luis Borges" just to enhance his own permanence.

- If I were Blount I would be concerned that authorship of the Borges statement—whose provenance is a long story that must go untold for reasons of national security and a woman's reputation—cannot be conclusively authenticated. To go down in a lump with Macpherson, "Shakespeare," Irving, Haley, Kosinski and McGinniss is barely preferable to not going down at all. To be sure, Macpherson *et al.* are not a law firm, but legal issues do arise, and the very detectability of Blount's stylistic influence on the text in question might be accounted for reductively in court.

- Certainly this apparent Borgesian acknowledgment of Blount's importance has been a long time surfacing, and I would say that misplacement or amanuensic envy, or a bit of both, is a plausible explanation.

For the record, I take no stance. I leave that to Blount. He is the historical figure. Perhaps less securely historical than he would like; but this revelation—for all of its rejection by the *National Enquirer*—may help. *I* don't care, I'm in it for the larks.

Actually, that's not true. We are in this together; we even occasionally intersect (that's as cosy as *I'm* going to get); and the answer to *what for* falls, to borrow Borges's expression, "through the cracks" (*por las salidas*).

I have to say, though: Blount is not exactly what I have in mind. Nothing about him (*pace* Borges) readily flows, including the name. *Blountian*. Unh. Rhymes more or less with *truncheon*. If the two of us have ever, in the true meaning of the word, been meant for each other, it is only in terms of some genetic code that I, for one, am at a loss to crack. Me, I'd go by Borges.

—I

9/31/93

Paul Bowles

Bowles and It

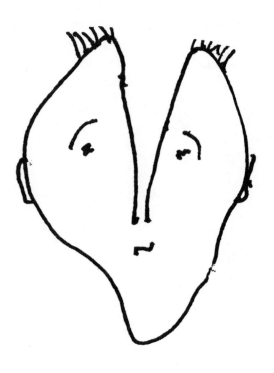

*W*hat is this curious assumption, widely shared (to judge from the extensive list of contributors to this issue) that *while writing,* a writer can identify himself as one who is writing? The consciousness of oneself as oneself causes a short circuit, and the light goes out.

If I am writing fiction, I am being invented. I cannot retain any awareness of identity. The two states of being are antithetical. The author is not at a steering wheel: "*I* am driving this car. *I* command its movements. *I* can make it go wherever *I* please." This assertion of identity is fatal; the writing at that point becomes meaningless.

What is *I*? It is indefinable, the basic prime number in the realm of words, dangerous and destructive. *I* is an unbounded magma of disparate words and images, an amalgam of the medicines I take daily; my personality is scattered over the tables and desks in my room. Catapressan, Cordaron, Torental, Neobrupen, Persantine, Clarityne, Passiflorine, Gentalline, Feldane, Homeoplasmine, KH3, Bactrim, Dacryoserum, Bacicoline, Chibroxine, Neutrogena, Hemovas, Inongan, Dilar, Zovirax, Pivalone, Synalar, Nasivine, Cidermex, Neosporin, Soluchrom. *I* is a whole, less than the sum of its pharmaceutical parts. My doppelganger is a list of products which I'm told keep me alive.

There are two questions here: Do they and am I?

Harold Brodkey

The One Who Writes

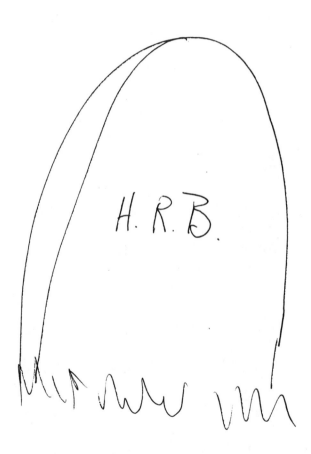

I am too delicate to have had a life. I am too easily interrupted. I have never had a real or outward life, never had anything to do with living or walking or seeing outwardly. I analyze those things—they fill me with wonder. I am suspended between eyes and hands and mind and paper among alphabetical squiggles and syllables—the hands are the hands of a robot. I am not a robot; I don't mean that. But when I work, the outside shell, that person is an automaton.

I am entirely suspended among a sense of sounds as heard in the head, not real sounds, but as if whispered, but very fast, a short-hand, short-ear, short-tongue. I have rarely, maybe only once or twice, if that, ever spoken to anyone, ever emerged in speech—at least, I have no sense of its having happened except at quiet eery moments when I was, in a way, sleepwalking. I did not know what I was doing.

A sense of sounds but not real sound, a sense of thoughts, but actual thinking is something some other self does, and while it is going on, it can't be written down. Usually, the outward self talks to someone or to himself. And whatever was thought moves blunderingly toward language and being written.

My playing field, my landscape, my entire reality is words, words in sequence, very rapid and aimed all ways, clustered and smoothed out, aimed at readers, and then, transcription, which is slow, and I am like a single held breath. Imagined events, imagined readers, imagined processes of work, of writing—I imagine myself finishing this paragraph before I begin it—are a real landscape if I am not ill or interrupted. I lose my real ears; they are useless. And my sense of taste doesn't register whatever the outer automaton chews on, including his own lip. I have no sense of the touch of the pen or the pencil or the keys of the machine or the color of the screen.

I have nearby selves who are aware if I wake to them, if I am dispersed, and one of them takes over. But me, I have only a startled sense of other people—I mean, entirely real, bodied people. Or of my outer self, or selves, the athletic one, the newspaper reading one, the one who learns to use machines. My awareness or awakening or their self-assertion, either one, is like a silent burst of fireworks or of some sort of artillery but the burst is sensory. Anyway, it murders me, disperses me, and this is so absolute that my separation from life is more than a harem-like imprisonment, more than is easily imagined: I cannot talk to people or run or see, and yet I am not a mole or a cripple . . . I have means of inner locomotion.

I have tried to lessen the separation. I have tried to stay concentrated and to live alongside or inside a living self. I have tried not to be dispersed, but it has never once worked. It seems large. It seems likely that the split between the privacy and the isolation is nearly absolute in the shadowy limbo of chutes and tunnels, perspectives and unreal woods in which I live. It is shadowy only in part. It lights up where I am. It lights up quite a lot if I imagine a general outdoor light.

My outer self, or selves in committee, that congress of worldly selves, creates me like a special counsel. Sometimes I tug at those outward powers, apply a faint or a choking tidal pull, but I have no power. My outer self is reluctant—afraid. Sometimes, like an older brother, it imitates me. It manifests a kind of choking half-dark will to be alone, to sleep alone, to have his dreams to himself—I mean it pursues an isolation that is parallel or analogous to mine. Sometimes it writes—and talks—in imitation. It is very strange, my dependent existence. I can pull away from the outer self with its wealth of attitudes into an eyeless daydreaming, but after just a second or two that outer congress has to allow this, has to be entertained. I am alone but enslaved, capable of all sorts of shadow feats, forced to work and yet I can really only work at my own volition. I am much weaker than a child. I have never really met or seen any-one's outer self, only an in-here version. I share memories and information with my outer selves, but only partially, very imper-fectly, in both directions. I have no power except that of curios-ity—and, to some extent, the power to amuse. Oh yes, pride. I have the power of pride. I am very largely a forbidden manifes-tation and unwise and unlikable when I work, someone to be teased. . . . My outer self has to indulge me, warm me, protect me, has to let me live and adjourn or kill itself for a while. Mus-cular restlessness or muscular wretchedness, the need to piss, almost any state other than hibernation and a certain degree of automatism in the surrounding congress disperses me, and I am done for until I am summoned, re-created, and then agree to work.

I can describe him in moonlight, relieved not to have to imagine the moonlight, not to have to phrase it, the silly moon-light, not to have to imagine the city street, the tight row of townhouses, the windows but to have it all be there, solidly there to the senses—he likes to be free of me. The unimagined world intoxicates that realer self, and I am—it is clear—a twist that his life has taken that he often dislikes.

I am dispersed by movement, by focusing my outer eyes. I

am easily dispersed. My world is imagined, but it is the only one I live in. I have around me a gulf of silence, a second or two of blankness—a distance—to wholeness. Everything in me is fractured and incomplete, is in small pieces that sometimes coalesce or that expand. In this citizenship, all is amusement and shape. Everything has a point, a clear purpose. Opinions are important, are final—for a while. Meaning is never absent; even meaninglessness is full of meaning here. I am, and I am in, some sort of simultaneous city of vistas of attention—ideas, words, and sentences in motion—oh, so many motions. I suppose not a million sentences but a million shadows of words, of syllables, whole New Yorks of half-written statements pour through me. . . . At times it seems I have a complete citizenship, an entire world, that the whole world is here in an unembodied way.

But that is an illusion. Gaps of absence, of omission quickly appear if I look for logical connections. It is all very stylized . . . very Manhattan, very Venetian. Something abrasive and nervous in this, some rebellious and unwise quality in this, rubs against the rest of me and erodes my outer self. My outer life often feels that the dramas and exertions of order, the emergencies and efforts of imagination of this inner Manhattan are shortening that outer life. And have ruined it and are ruining it more. For me to work seems reckless and lonely, peninsular.

Now that my outer self is ill and tires easily, I am a respite from that. But I am weaker, too, and when I begin to come to the end of what I can do for the day, the outer world bursts on me more gently than it used to. It begins to announce itself as daytime or nighttime brightness of colors, of objects, and of sounds—tangible, all of it so that the word *place* as it springs up reflects forward and back, reflects the inhabited word—the word inhabited by what is visible, not to me, but to my outer self—I merely remember this—and reflects itself, *place* and desk and lamp burning and stereo playing, colors and surfaces, reality, nothing silly and illogical like the paragraphs I have been writing. Nothing like moonlight. Merely a room.

But I am almost present in it, almost present alongside my outer self. I have never had a life in any usual sense, but I will have a death.

Cecil Brown

There's a Black Man Imprisoned in Me

*C*ecil, brotherman, m'boy, mah main man, my ace-bone coon, is one educated dude. He speaks German. But me, I can't even remember how to say good morning in English. So I just say fuck you to everybody. Cecil is a smart brother. Now me, I'm a stone stomp-down brother in Black. I mean . . . it's night and day between us. He is a writer of intellect, but me . . . hey . . . I'm an oral person, I'm illiterate. I'm MC ID and DJ Superego; without his help I couldn't even read our name. I'm zipcoon, and he's the NooNegro.

But don't jump to conclusions. I have something he doesn't have. I have *motherwit*. He went to college and studied all about white civilization, okay? He was exposed to white civilization, okay? When he goes to these interracial meetings, he knows how to act. Me, I just act like I always act . . . like a nigger. Like I'd say whuzup. He'll say, "Hello." See what I mean? I'll begin a sentence with "Like" or "You dig?" or "You know what I'm sayin'?" He would *never* do that. We are doing the same thing, but we say it differently. Sometimes when he is having a hard time thinking of something to say, he will turn and ask me to get him started. I do. I be doin mah thanz, muthahumper.

Check this out. We went to this faculty party for Christmas, okay? I was hungry, but he wouldn't eat 'cause he had this conversation going on with Professor Longnose, who was with this swanky white witch named Tuesday. I embarrassed the shit out of Cecil when I made a remark about the size of her breasts. I slipped the message into a remark Cecil was making about the influence of ragtime on Eugene O'Neill.

Professor Longnose asked Cecil, "Where do you come from?"

"I was born in 1943, North Carolina," sezzee, "in a small, tobacco-farming town called Bolton and grew up the eldest in a family of seven." For as long back as any of them could remember, he went on, telling his life story, his people earned their living from working in the fields.

But *my* ancestors were the *real* field slaves, his were the house servants, but he likes to take on *my history* when he's talking to white folks. But I don't say anything. I just let him talk. To embarrass him, I keep staring at Tuesday's assets with an overly obvious interest. Needless to say, Professor Longnose got upset.

"Excuse me," sezzee (Professor Longnose), "but I must be going. It was nice talking with you."

Miss Tuesday of the Big Ones smiles at Cecil. "It was my pleasure!" She winked and whispered, "I like zee way you observe *everything!*"

Cecil said, "Did I say the wrong thing?"

I said, "I slipped a misunderstanding in your meaning, man."

"Do you know what a nigger is?" I asked him.

"No," sezzee.

"A nigger is the gentleman that just left the conversation."

Which made him laugh. We create stories out of this process. My embarrassment *inspires* him to create a story. He is too nice a guy to embarrass anybody. He is the *proper* Negro who is ashamed of me, the nigger. Yet when he is writing late at night, and the stilted proper English ain't flowing, guess who he calls on? He wants me to "express" myself for him in my slang, my vernacular. The sucker "steals" my language and robs me of my spontaneity. My only recourse is to cuss him out.

By my cussing him out constantly, playing Caliban to his Prospero, and by his masking my cry against our oppression, we create a peculiar narrative. If you wanted to go all out you could call it "authentic."

He told me, sezzee, you are my Black prisoner. He is my guard. So of course, like Caliban, I let him twist my interjections into pleasant phrases, which, apparently, amuse others who buy his books. I get no respect. And if somebody sends me something in the way of praise, he intercepts it like a guard, sniffs through it, like Snoop Doggy Dogg, eats it if he is hungry (he is always hungry). If I get a visitor, he begrudges me that. Racists oppress *him* and he oppresses *me*. I am his Black brother, savage, exotic, barbaric. . . .

What's that?

Yeah, you are right. I oppress him? Yes, yes, out of this double—excuse me—*triple* oppression comes my narrative style.

Rosellen Brown

Who Is the Reader in That

Ring of Light?

Here's the real R.B.

*S*o it is a myth, then, that I bought into through all my years of innocence and hunger: that I write to bridge the abyss between myself and others; that I long to make friends of strangers, share secrets, seek and offer solace with my words alone.

A safe ideal when my readers were more theoretical than actual, numbered by their absence, which was gigantic, overpowering. Now, by an accident of subject and marketing (and only marginally, I fear, by skill), my book is in half a million hands or more and suddenly—how strange, how unanticipated, how scaffolded with paraphernalia—that "I" feels simultaneously adopted and orphaned, manhandled and abandoned. Perversity!

It is suddenly considered necessary to show a photograph of me cooking dinner with my husband so that, coast to coast, readers of the most popular magazine in airplanes and doctors' waiting rooms can contemplate the frying pan over which we confer. A "literary escort," her meter ticking, holds up my book, my face, to the disembarking passengers at the airport; I claim her or, rather, she claims me; I go forth in her iron grip to hawk myself at the kind of bookstore I love to cruise around anonymously. The "I" who put those words in a quadrille-lined note-book in black ink, three words forward, four words back, is pro-foundly embarrassed by having to claim them now so confi-dently and hides behind the pile of books on the table, refusing to listen to hear if the cash register's ringing. That "I" talks too much, offers too many intimate details of composition, of inten-tion and hope, more than anyone's asked for, trying to re-create the reality that this book has anything to do with her.

Letters arrive, announcing that my book has inaugurated a new era in the family: détente. Talk. Confession of ancient pain. I have become, willy-nilly, a therapist. An anguished woman phones. She has lost a chunk of her past and is convinced she has found it in my novel, certain she was present in one scene. "Did you ever live in Albany? Did you know the Hamiltons?" I protest vigorously, try to defend the idea of fiction, speak about the imagination, but she continues, desperate. "Did that house have double glass doors at the back? A pool?" My characters are present at her seance; I am a spectator.

Thus, by their neediness, their curious approaches, and their sheer love—my own kind of love—of *the word,* idea of the word, which they generously make flesh, I feel, finally, like a sweater tangled on a counter in Filene's basement, soiled with fingerprints, lifted and dropped again, picked up by someone else (with better taste), paid for, bagged.

But if I did not offer myself for sale, then what am I doing here?

I have disappeared from this adventure, not bitter, mind you, only nonplussed by the ultimate irrelevance of an audience to the process of writing. I thought I wrote so as not to be alone—a social impulse, comradely, for animal warmth—but *this* isn't it at all. This noise is alternately rich and tinny. The true reverberations turn out to be only internal, and against the echo of easy applause I have to struggle, now, to hear them. You write for yourself, I have always told students and audiences—

for the "it," Eudora Welty called it—and you are the ultimate judge of what is pleasing, fit, necessary. But now I know it is only when you catch a crowd listening that you discover how lonely you actually love to be, sitting protectively on those words like a bird on a nest. You see the little self that holds the pen cower in darker dark than ever. The name on the best-seller list, on the rack at the supermarket, is spelled like yours, yet, as if it were a crime you committed in a dream, you would deny responsibility if you could; you hardly feel complicit. You have long since fled a scene made of such alien public gestures, and in too much light.

When I was a teenager I used to think about august figures making love—beyond visualizing, my teacher! the president! of course, my parents! Later I realized that the truly intimate scene, far more impossible to imagine, was not the act of sex but the act of imaginative creation: that noisy storyteller alone at her desk chewing on her pencil. That flirtatious poet at midnight turned to himself as to a wall.

Now what I want to envision is the single reader I began with in my earliest dreams. She, he, is sitting in a large chair in yellow light, silently turning the pages I have apparently invented and filled, maybe sipping a cup of coffee from a heavy mug, as I do. My dear old "I" slips out of its dark corner, then, to watch and listen to the occasional quickened intake of breath. This is what I wished for. I realize that the person in the fat, enveloping chair, whose face is hidden, is myself.

So much for solidarity with the world. Readers are good and necessary accomplices, but I see they are only stand-ins for myself. I want to replenish the well of words out of which I've drunk happily all my life, yes, but like a greedy child I seem to be thinking, ungenerously, "For me, for me!" I am, finally, not eager to save a single soul, or even to lure forth admiration or conversation. Written or read, it is all the same. I am only eager to close the door and be alone with my book.

Robert Olen Butler

Butler and I

Butler is not an intellectual. He is a sensualist. Even my saying just this much that is abstract makes him restless. He moves me to the inner window ledge in this hotel room in Miami where his work has brought me and I sit on it and lean against the glass and I look out at Biscayne Bay wrinkling like the instep of the foot of a woman with russet hair and I feel her on my fingertips and on the point of my hip and on my tongue though she is two days past now, from another hotel in another place, with sounds of the street, and now I have the hiss of this silent room with the water far below me and soon I am before a hundred people and I read what Butler has written. It is I who read, I come to his words as I come to the window ledge, to learn from him, to shut down my mind which is too comfortable, always, which holds me away from the things Butler wants to take in—needs to take in—to do what he must do, shape these words that I read now before the lifted faces and she lifts her face to me as soon as the door is shut behind us and her eyes are russet too and all this I know from Butler because he created this woman even before I met her and I am upon a time with these hundred who hear him and they are all very still even as I pause and listen to them listening and I listen too and when I am done, they ask me questions, ask me to rationally explain Butler. I try: there is no art without first a forgetting, there is no art where the effect precedes the writing, there is no art that is not sought every day, there is no art apart from the senses (even at this, which he believes in perhaps the most, Butler is turning restless at the terms of this discourse, the working of the mind). There is no art without courage. Kurosawa said that to be an artist means never to avert your eyes, and now Butler whispers to me to follow that advice, to stop talking like this, and I do, I sit and sign his books and I feel the hands that I shake and I do not miss the tear-bright eyes of a man who says he was in Vietnam and I know he loved a woman there and then I return to my window ledge, on my own, and Butler is pleased at this and the hotel room is full of the deep night hum of Manhattan and Butler's face is wet with the desire of the woman we love, and we are one, the three of us.

Frank Conroy

Me and Conroy

Frank Conroy

*H*e needs me more than I need him, but you'd never know it from the way he treats me. Contempt is perhaps too strong a word. It's something icier, more distant, more perfectly disinterested. He uses me as if I could quite easily be replaced, which is certainly not true. Not easily, anyway. Who else would put up with him the way I have? (For instance, this is the fourth version of this particular manuscript and it's only a tiny bit better than the first. A lot of time for a very small gain, in other words, and no complaints will be heard.) Who else would ask nothing of him—and I mean nothing, not once, ever—simply for the experience of his company? What makes it worse is I think he knows all this and finds it banal. Yes! He does! I felt it just now as my hand wrote the word.

Should I mention the matter of the cigarettes? I think I should. After smoking a pack a day for forty years I stopped five months ago. Quitting was extremely difficult, to say the least, but the support of my family and friends helped. I'm on the verge of a big change here, which is to say seeing myself as a nonsmoker, accepting myself as a nonsmoker. Everybody respects this except him. My abstinence irritates him for some reason, and when I try to write he tempts me with images of the red and gold Dunhill package, which he knows I used to smoke on special occasions. "Is this not a special occasion?" he seems to be saying, "with the clipboard across your knees and your pen in your hand? Is this not as special as it's ever going to get?" Arrogant bastard.

You see, there's nothing fancy about it. The situation resembles the basic story line of a thousand execrable country-western songs more than it does any delicate Borgesian aperçu. I've laid my life on the line, and if that isn't love I don't know what love is. For my entire adult life he has simply popped up whenever it pleased him, used me, put me through a million changes, and split without warning, leaving me exhausted and enervated. He takes me, and my love, entirely for granted and if I had any brains I'd tell him to fuck off. But of course it's far too late for that. He is my fate, for better or worse.

I just wish he'd talk to me directly sometime. You know, stop whatever he's doing and look me in the eye and tell me something that would help me get rid of this idea of myself as some feckless brokenhearted jukebox cowboy crying in my beer. I mean would the sky fall? Would the stars freeze in their courses? God damn it, he owes me. Don't you think?

Guy Davenport

Keeping Time

GUY DAVENPORT

"*B*orges y Yo," which seems to observe with Borgesian gloom that the coin outlasts the emperor, is also a Borgesian co-nundrum, for Borges the writer necessarily wrote it, not the *yo* of its title. Wittgenstein worried about who the *my* is when we say, "My foot hurts." We say, "I am writing," not "My hand is writing." How much of us has the ego colonized? When was Shakespeare a playwright, all the time? Proust said that we are not ourselves all the time, and not all of ourselves at any time.

A philosopher has suggested that there is no such thing as a mind; we have instead various ganglia of consciousness in communication with each other. This would account for Socra-tes' belief in a *daimon* (Latin, *genius*). The daimon seems as good an explanation as any of the writer's (and the world's) sense that there was something more to the limber-legged Irish-man than the wayward citizen James Joyce. The Borges duet was an Argentine librarian and his daimon.

Daimons, Plutarch tells us, are laundered and polished souls of the dead, sent back to guide those who will give them heed. My daimon (we're great pals) was a minor poet in the au-tumn of Roman time, polite, bashful, and pensive. *His* daimon, however, had been a charming lout too comfortable with himself to amount to anything but a joy to his enemies and a nuisance to his friends. So when I write I am disorganized by my daimon's daimon, but kept in order by my daimon himself.

Socrates' daimon was an inheritance from the Pythagoreans. All of our daimons are personifications of the past, which is the ground beneath our feet. The more diligent the writer, the deeper back into the past he can reach. The old Tolstoy became a contemporary of the prophet Amos. Joyce in *Finnegans Wake* speaks from the bogs, through mists. Centuries intervened between the war in Troy and Homer.

My daimon is both a pest and an obliging teacher. His language is Latin, though he admires Greek. Tidy your sentences. If you're going to write English, write it idiomatically. Be as plain as you can, but don't leave anything out. Of English writers he is forever holding up John Bunyan, Ben Jonson, and Samuel Butler. Sugar the biscuit if you must, he says, but make certain that you have a biscuit to sugar.

He holds his Roman nose at the idea of writing as self-expression. Writing is our finest implement of inquiry, and the inquirer inquiring into himself is a mirror held up to a mirror. The business of a writer is to show others how you see the world so that they will then have two views of it, theirs and yours. We are all of us trapped in our minds. We can get out through the imaginative alchemy of reading, a skill complementary to writing but psychologically more mysterious. How writing is written is far more straightforward a process than how it is read. Leave that to them, my daimon says, when I doubt a sentence.

My daimon likes to say that only I can write my stories, and has refused to have anything to do with this miniature essay on "the authorial I." It has no weather in it, no apples in a silver bowl, no goats with oblong eyes. *Taedium taurique stercus,* he says. So I have had to write this all by myself.

John Fowles

The J.R. Fowles Club

(1948)

*T*he "J.R. Fowles" is the name of the club to which I belong, for my sins. A number, indeed most, of its numerous other members consider they barely do. Indeed, we're generally treated as sheer deadwood—mere ciphers on some wretched mailing list, recipients of obscure requests for charity, badly written annual bulletins (mostly about people we can't even remember), invitations to nauseating reunion dinners (for which we have to pay ourselves, natch) . . . I'm sure you'll all be only too familiar with this sort of horror and its ghastly vacuities. As for the wretched president, Sir John Eye, and the never-available secretary, Mr Mee, honestly . . . how the damned thing staggers on at all defeats reality. I certainly never asked to join it, and often wish I hadn't. I suspect my father, attracted by the name, foolishly put me down for it before I was born. Quite a lot of my fellow-members will hardly exchange a civil word; others do nothing but whine and whinge. Yet others (talk about egos!) are self-important beyond belief, especially one fathead who fancies himself a novelist. Another pretends to be a feminist. I'd like to see him just once with a duster or an iron in his hand. Another pair both think they know everything about natural history—one a sort of scientist, the other a sort of poet. You can imagine. They never bump into each other without a god-awful slanging match. That's typical, I'm afraid. Nothing that comes before the so-called management committee—aesthetic, moral, political, domestic, you name it—*ever* gets a *nem. con.* vote. We are truly an unspeakably futile shambles. I honestly shall resign, if they don't watch out. I've always hated men's clubs, anyway.

Paula Fox

Path

I cannot write of writing. To be at work, to write, must exclude thoughts about writing or about myself as a writer. To consider writing, to look at myself as a writer, holds for one sober moment, then plunges me into a tangle of misery that Cesare Pavese describes in his diary: "This terrible feeling that what you do is all wrong, so is what you think, what you are!"

It all suggests to me Heisenberg's indeterminacy principle, which states that you can either know where a thing is or how fast it is moving—but not both simultaneously. The warring self disappears into the self-less concentration of work. Imagination is conjunctive and unifying; the sour, habitual wars of the self are disjunctive and separating.

When I begin a story at my desk, the window to my back, the path is not there. As I start to walk, I make the path.

William H. Gass

Pierre Menard and Me

PIERRE M. GASS

*B*orges does not know who is writing this page. It is I, Pierre Menard, his own creation, who, since it's my turn now, writes his name, my Spanish a mot Frenchy like a curling corner. 'Tis I who follow his words like a trail through the forest. 'Tis I who bring life to Borges because some reader has bothered to become Menard. Bored, I have given up my recomposition of *Don Quixote.* It was, although a task which seemed endless, too easy, the sense of each sentence as vast yet open as a plain. The Don was too derivative, too, having fallen from some forgotten limb of the *Arabian Nights* like fruit from a tree. Instead, I have decided to compose a brief piece entitled "Borges and I." It will be a word-for-word match of Borges's original, so you might think it but a copy; however, I shall put a bit more of myself between the lines than Borges was inclined to. And since Pierre Menard will sign his name, confessing that it's his work really, the sense of every word will change. Moreover, Borges left his words like last breaths. My eye makes mine as fresh each dawn as newly risen bread. Borges, Pierre Menard, and me: a piece as briefly perfect as a crocus. So far I've accomplished one sentence, one sentence which feels like a phrase: *all things long to persist in their being . . .*

Each of us is a Pierre Menard, of course, for Pierre was—he is—a multiple fellow, not simply a snobby minor symbolist. He is any you or I inclining his or her attention to the page, composing my or your lines like his in her head: you saying *all things long* and feeling near death; I reading *all things long* and licking my lips; she seeing *all things long* and reading "we all wish"; nevertheless, though I am Pierre Menard now and then, Menard is not me. To me belongs the blind glance of the poet. Lunch was beginning like a puppet play, small cloths unfolding with a flourish to cover lap and knees. Ah, Borges said, hearing my name with a courteous attention me assumed was customary, yours is not an ordinary name. Me admitted this. He had, I thought, hands heavy from their burden of always watching where they were: between spoon and saucer now, at the linen's edge. I am curious, Borges pretended, what does your name mean? It means me, was my first thought. It is a German name, not Scots as some think. Not Scots, Borges murmured, as if that had been his presumption. No, it's from the German and means small street or alley. Does it? does it? Borges said with polite excitement. His right hand crawled across the table toward me. Does it? Ah . . . you know mine—Borges—is derived from Burgos, a city. Then his interest went out like a paper match.

I am considering, in my composition of "Borges and I," how to describe Borges's attempt to escape from Borges, the way his eye had already eluded what it might have seen: a page of his own prose, perhaps, a line about transparent tigers and towers of blood, the configuration of pieces in a game of chess, an alley without a destination. Shall I imply that the failure of his flight affirms his reluctant identity? and that of the flawed with the flawless?

We spoke of the talk he was about to give, of his interest in the Eddas, Iceland, and the Norse, of Snorri Sturluson (for there was a name!), and of the pleasure Borges took in distant ideas, faintly resonating strings. I knew that I, in all I said, could be no more than the eager foolish me I was. Menard's conjecture was correct. *Long . . .* to *long . . .* was the initially recovered word of his new work. To be called "Borges and I." And now it was time for Borges and me to leave for his lecture, which me would introduce. He sat suddenly back in his drawn-out chair, and a glorious wide smile wrinkled his face. Ah, he said, you see, you see . . . I am a city . . . and you are an alley. That did indeed, me thought, sum it up.

And what did his pun prove? that Borges had always been Borges, and had lived in third persons like a populace. All things, as Spinoza said, stubbornly resist the long division of their being. I knew I would always remain Menard, though remaining me, while reading Borges, content to be a modest, possibly pointless alley in his lucent yet labyrinthine city, with no desire to divide my reading "I" from that of Pierre Menard, or to withdraw, from Jorge Luis Borges, his small place in town for me.

Gail Godwin

The Girl in the Basement

Gail Godwin

"One more thing," said the interviewer. "Could you give me the names of all the high schools you attended, with dates?"

No I couldn't. There were six schools in four years, and that whole era of my life had a Missing in Action quality about it. I told the interviewer I'd get back to her and descended to my basement files. Reading for the first time through a fat packet of my teenage letters, faithfully saved and generously returned several years ago by my oldest friend, I excavated not only the requested dates but, as they say, "much, much more!"

Not only was an astonishing portion of the missing daily action restored to me, but I think I located the point in my chronology where all this got serious: the moment when a fifteen-year-old Gail, writing a letter in red ink to a best friend left behind in another town, suddenly distances herself from the personal chronicle and enters an entirely new mode. In the middle of a paragraph, the hyperactive, desperately upbeat, merry-go-round prose of high school social calendar, parental frictions, and boy aches is abruptly stilled into this:

. . . I can hear the dead leaves on Mr. Speer's mimosa tree rattling. An airplane just flew over the house as usual. Somebody shuffled a deck of cards downstairs. A baby is crying in one of the apartments. Another airplane. It is not quite eight but black as pitch outside. All I can see is [sic] a few squares of light where people's houses are and WAIM's big radio tower with red lights. It is the first time I have really been lonely and yet it doesn't hurt too much. At least I have windows to look out of, and a pen and some notebook paper and a friend who'll listen to all this soap opera.

I held it in my hands, I sneezed from its dust: a forty-two-year-old red inkling of how the chronic, self-circling "I" performs an early act of mutating into the impersonal roving Eye. The Eye swings outward experimentally into the surrounding darkness, questing, registering, plundering the signs and signals of others ("a few squares of light"), then homes back like an excited fledgling to spill its trophies into the maw of the waiting intelligence, who organizes the small bounty into communicable shape and passes it on to a friendly reader.

I'm not sure the process ever really changes much. Oh, the flights out the window get longer and more sustained, and, one hopes, more swoopingly daring and bountiful. One's style, gradually stripped of apologies and posings, becomes one's own. The only thing that has changed for me is the *why* of doing it. At the start, when I was the girl in plaid shorts with the red ink, being dragged to all those new towns by the people who thought they owned me, I made the "I"-to-Eye excursions to flee bedevilment and frustration. Escaping my prosaic self, in small spurts, revealed itself as a heady method of temporary salvation. I somehow discovered, perhaps on that very night of Mr. Speer's clacking mimosa leaves, that if I "went out the window" for awhile and came back and described it, I could make myself less desperate. Later on, the flights evolved from practice runs into habit and, eventually, into mainline necessity. At some point the excursions became my most comfortable element, my true domicile. Now I can't "just stay home" anymore if I try, however unbedeviled and attractive that place of residence has become. I haven't been able to be simply myself for decades. Like the vampire, if you like, I must be constantly venturing abroad to gorge on lives that are not mine.

The present life of my chronic "I," with its diurnal round of dates and places and pleasures and woes, continues to spin, much as it did in the old red-ink days. But from the point of view of the Flying Eye that inveterately lures me out again into its nightbaths of otherness, it sometimes seems as if I'm already haunting my own completed file, closed and neatly labeled and quietly gathering dust in its basement corner.

"So then what happens to our great 'Flying Eye' when we die?" the girl in the plaid shorts wants to know.

It's a good question and I respect her too much to euphemize or equivocate. "I think it probably goes on . . . doing what it does."

"But then how can it have been *ours?* And what were we to it? I mean, did it save us or finish us?"

"Probably both. Would you have had it any different?"

"I'm not sure I had any *choice!*"

"Well, exactly," I say.

Edward Gorey

A Penchant for Pseudonyms

*A*bout the time my first book was published over forty years ago I found my name lent itself to an edifying number of anagrams, some of which I've used as pen names, as imaginary authors, and as characters in their or my books. A selection of examples follows.

Ogdred Weary has written *The Curious Sofa,* a pornographic work, and *The Beastly Baby,* a book no one wanted to publish.

Mrs. Regera Dowdy, who lived in the nineteenth century, is the author of *The Pious Infant* and such unwritten works as *The Rivulets of Gore* and *Nets to Subdue the Deranged;* she also translated *The Evil Garden* by Eduard Blutig, the pictures for which were drawn by O. Müde.

Madame Groeda Weyrd devised the Fantod Pack of fortune-telling cards.

Miss D. Awdrey-Gore was a celebrated and prolific mystery story writer (*The Toastrack Enigma, The Blancmange Tragedy, The Postcard Mystery, The Pincushion Affair, The Toothpaste Murder, The Dustwrapper Secret, The Teacosy Crime,* etc.); her detective is Waredo Dyrge, whose favourite reading is the Dreary Rewdgo Series for Intrepid Young Ladies (*D.R. on the Great*

Divide, D.R. in the Yukon, D.R. at Baffin Bay, etc.) by Dewda Yorger.

Dogear Wryde's work appears only on postcards.

Addée Gorrwy is known as the Postcard Poetess.

Wardore Edgy wrote movie reviews for a few months.

Wee Graddory was an Infant Poet of an earlier century.

Dora Greydew, Girl Detective, is the heroine of a series (*The Creaking Knot, The Curse on the Sagwood Estate,* etc.) by Edgar E. Wordy.

Garrod Weedy is the author of *The Pointless Book.*

Agowy Erderd is a spirit control.

However, I am still taken aback whenever someone asks me if that indeed is my real name.

Allan Gurganus

The Fertile "We" of One Chaste "I"

actual writer →

AUTHOR

"*H*ow *is a lawyer like a single sperm?" They each have about one chance in a hundred and fifty million of becoming human.*"

Start with the awesome erection of one upright "I." A long shot, all of it.

As the public gasbag "author," I remain outwardly colorful, personable, regional, dogged, left-leaning if well-dressed, raffish, opinionated on behalf of keeping lazier interviewers happy. As the cringing, self-critical, hyper-private "writer," I myself remain the color of, say, lint. *That's* the artist.

Lint, until I am alone at home, till I slip into something more uncomfortable, the rich disguise of others' anguish, their dainty wasting erotic obsessions, their unaccountable ambitions; till I, through that, achieve opacity and force, till I again become—while perfectly alone—almost personal again.

"The author" lives in revolt against the middle-class conditioning that warned us we must never call attention to ourselves, never exaggerate or overdramatize, never complain or whine. So "the author" drinks too much, he sure abuses credit cards, he shoots up with shared and sticky needles, he pinches all attractive, youthful men and women within reach, as much to gauge their sweet, shocked expressions as for some later pay-off at the hotel, Room 703, any time.

"The writer" is merely a day-job bank teller. Visored in green, safe behind the brass grille of First National Bank, he stays locked inside the mandatory white shirt, black tie, safe-sealed behind thick glasses. He spends his 9–5 peeling off other people's denominations of dreams, giving back to them what they themselves have long since misered aside. And so deserve.

What interests me about my own work and character is not the solid, admirable, good-nurse, self-motivated persona that I simulate toward Frans Hals warmth in scholarly talks, in photographs taken during charity banquets. That guy is about as real as his tweed jacket's suede elbow patches and about that necessary. It's Lint Man I'm a slave for. Poor dweeb hasn't had a date since 1965; and hasn't regretted that since January 1972.

He, the true writer, is the department store dummy at the very center of the whole establishment, the one left alone on display all night, a price tag stapled to every piece of clothing they've yanked onto him, binoculars and frog flippers included. He is the neutral, generic human form, the gray center who must always assume disguises—in order to be seen and, therefore, to feel, himself. He flings heroic motives onto ignoble persons (and vice versa). Terrified of heights, he still rushes up the glass mountains of Grand Opera's swooniest states. He lies History.

This inward, unsure, tender, professional empathizer is a man far older and even balder than I. He's myopic and a stutterer and yet (while alone in his rental efficiency with its one hot plate and radio), unlikely as it seems, just by pulling a Spanish shawl over his right shoulder, Lint Man becomes the aggrieved, outrageous, stunning Señorita; Lint Man gimping toward the bed reverts to War Veteran; Lint Man, losing a dime, is suddenly the wailing mother of a child taken early. Love and trust precisely this shy, marginal, small-town employee. His emotional quicksand yields the endless marble identities. This artist is slightly blind, a bureaucratic, slope-shouldered bachelor whose birthday no one remembers. I sing how gladly he gives everything away to his Adored, his too-sexual, beauty-loving characters caught between History's long raw deal and Comedy's brief kickbacks.

How lavish and how Godlike is Lint Man's open-endedness, Lint Man's specificity. Of all the fictional lives I've ever tried inventing, *his* remains hardest to know. He is that favorite toy of boys today: The Transformer. Proteus again. Lint Man, a wimp to the naked eye, has the real winner in his pants, the ever-upright deacon "I"—source of all seminal ideas, gusher goal of the size queens, God's own nephew gopher—Lint Man, the unpromoted First National teller. He is Tillich's God: "the ground of our being."

Just one more ragged, struggling, whiptail sperm, gone—blind—in search of the egg's sweet sushi consolations. It's this bald microscopic overcompensator I love most. Love most and therefore sing best.

The chances of achieving literary permanence are, to the decimal point, exactly the odds against becoming fully human.

That means one hundred and fifty million to one.

Which means one hundred and fifty million in one.

Jim Harrison

Squaw Gulch

*A*n hour's walk meant two hours of cutting cockleburrs out of the hair of the English setter, Tess, with my moustache scissors. On this walk in Squaw Gulch near Patagonia, Arizona, I was catching up to what I had become, but failing to reach the outline of my back fading into the umbrous, twilit canyon. We are always well ahead of where we think we are. Finding yourself, in total, where you actually are could be dangerous except, of course, in writing where you may only be a few seconds behind. Without writing the experience frequently brings on vertigo and sudden death. When on the verge of this frightening event I usually fall back to my position well before birth when I was just another ordinary citizen in one of the Black Holes bandied about by astronomers these days. How could these nitwits presume we were unaware of our ancestral home?

After the cockleburr surgery I drive to the Big Steer Tavern for a couple of whiskeys. Most surgeons require a little sedation after gore. There is a disturbing image of a rockpile in a bedroom in a fallen-down farmhouse years ago. A man regularly slept on this rockpile, and there is evidence that he also coupled with his sisters there. Once while hunting grouse and woodcock I inspected this not very ancient ruin and found the madman's poetry in a small metal box. On reading a few pages my brain crackled like ice. Words fail me now. Suffice it to say there was the sound of a pig being butchered, a rabbit hit by an owl, the lost lament of Kitty Genovese. Here was a man who lived in a previously undescribed world, a man who had fully caught up with himself. I returned the pages to the metal box and fled.

Of course we all feel poignantly that reality is a bourgeois creation. There have been those hallowed nights, cherished and feared, when our minds whirled throughout the universe far from the safety of this mediocre creation. Laing said that the mind of which we are unaware is aware of us. The distance we decide to establish in between is a matter of good sense and usually makes for better marriages and picnics, but not necessarily better art.

There is the old Haida notion that you are what comes to you and what you choose to fulfill. It is not enough to count coup on ghosts who are anyway still as alive as we are. The morning's paper said an old man, blind and deaf since 1945, had died totally without identity. Perhaps he was a true Taoist.

And perhaps tomorrow I'll awake at dawn with a gutful of courage, ready to fully inhabit the earth with a pen sharp as a fence post. In contrast to this calling, merging with wolves, bears and women has been child's play, which is the best kind, certainly far superior to the overexamined life. Perception without myth is mere description, the difference between probing the soul-life of the undescribed reality and picking our own lice. It is the hardest thing we have to remember, and doubtless the thing we shall never stop forgetting.

Meanwhile, back at an actual ranch, our otherness beckons, pulls, tears at us. Stavrogin is always biting Kirilov's ear, and vice versa. We are blessed because we can become ten thousand things. We are as ancient as dogs and brave enough to admit that on certain days the sun is upside down.

John Hawkes

Hawkes and Hawkes

I will not soon forget the day, very nearly the hour, when, about forty years ago, a young man asked me how I felt being a writer, an identity I disclaimed then and still do. In fact I was appalled by the question. Even in my earliest youth I knew, if only by intuition, that the writer and person in whom the writer existed were not at all one and the same. Even then, as his spokesman, I insisted on his detachment, his cruelty, his refusal to accept ordinary human values. I myself, on the other hand, was innocent—above all, innocent, and still am, no matter what I have done to destroy it. Hand in hand with my remarkable innocence went kindness, even sweetness of temperament, good nature, honesty (behind which I had to admit that I detected the writer's dishonesty). Here I should mention that my writer's voice emerged from my own mouth, on stage, as a voice of immense power, immense humor, with the ability to awe and manipulate audiences. As the mere man harboring the writer, I enjoyed his performance. If in quiet moments someone read aloud a few sentences of mine, I rarely recognized them and, on hearing the author named—myself—I began to feel the pride that was generally alien to myself as husband, father, friend. I was naive, and pleased when at last I came to admit to that characteristic. But why did I so disclaim the writer that neither I nor circumstances could annihilate? Because of vanity. I knew, with ever increasing certitude, that my writer, that every writer, weighs as much on the scale of "how to be" as the person he consumes. And doesn't the writer sometimes, like the octopus, cloud the actuality of his living person? He does. Rare is the writer who does not eventually drown his counterpart in the black ink of vanity. Here, as earlier, I should add that my writer's voice has assumed, on the page, many personae—that of Nazi, adulterer, even a horse, to name but a few of my narrators. Behind each one remains the voice of the writer.

Some time ago I discovered that I could no longer speak aloud or read aloud from a stage, even for the sake of hearing the effect that my writer's voice produced on listeners. Now, curiously, the more I try merely to live, the more reclusive I become, the vainer I am. At last I am as vain as the one who incessantly voices his silence inside me.

Mark Helprin

....

Helprin and I

The Author (left), with E. E. Cummings (Right, seated), and Lillian Hellman (center) at a mountain holiday, Gstaad (is that spelled correctly?), 1937. Underneath the table is the Gore Vidal.

*A*s the fox lies panting in the brush he paints a vivid picture of what surrounds him. Sounds, smells, vibration, interrupted light, even how the air moves: All print upon the quick fox mind images of his private war. Aping the fox, I tell you what follows.

When the Queen of England speaks in the first person plural, it sounds marvelously schizoid, and probably is for her a deep embarrassment. When an American politician has gone around the bend, he begins to refer to himself in the third person. All people feel that they are more than one. Even an Eskimo who returns from the ice to sit in the shadows inside an igloo must sometimes ask himself what the hunt has done to him, must wonder why his tenderness with his children takes so long to flood back after his sinews have been bent and frozen hard in the chase. It happens to everyone and to all of us, and only the crazed and the privileged permit themselves the luxury of disintegration into more than one self.

What privilege allows a writer to play Ping-Pong with himself (or even doubles tennis)? The unprecedented enrichment of the developed economies in the past century. In this period for the first time in history most writers—the good, the bad, and the ugly—have done nothing but write. They even go to writing school before they start to write. Writing is now a profession, much like brokering stocks or lawyering. It is no longer a relief from one's profession. Enter fatigue, boredom, repetition, responsibility. Furthermore, you tend to write about what you know. Melville wrote about whales, Emily Dickinson wrote about the soul, and today's writers write about themselves. When it was not a profession there was no need to escape it, for it itself was the escape.

However many of me there are, I have managed to fuse them into one. I cannot tell myself apart any more than the heavily breathing fox hiding under branches or in brush perceives in the mirror of his wide and alert eye a new dainty self or a different sad self or an admirably reflective self. As long as he feels death above him and he hears the hounds and the air is cold all selves are beaten into one—the runner, the listener, the thinker, the leaper. All his metals are laid, one strip upon the other, red hot, and as the blacksmith's hammer strikes, it knows only a single piece of steel.

Let the Queen of England say and suffer "we," and politicians imprisoned in the ether of self-regard refer to themselves as if to another, and writers in the Argentine reflect upon their intertwining double lives. As for me, I can't even break myself apart when I try. But it's not as simple as it appears, and do you know why? Because a fox wrote this, not I.

Alice Hoffman

Labrador Retriever Wishes He Could Tell All

*O*ur author never makes public appearances. If she agreed to give a reading, she would stumble over the unfamiliar prose she takes credit for. If she dared consent to an interview, she'd be hard pressed to distinguish between the plot of her first novel and her most recent book.

Early on, I hoped that someone would discover my situation, even rescue me. I sat by the front door, waiting in vain for a critic, a journalist, anyone who would reveal the truth. I grew to despise the postman, the only one who ever had occasion to venture onto our front porch. Back then, my dreams were still filled with silly things—rabbits, games of fetch, ducks sound asleep in the tall grass. My predecessors, two German Shepherds, who tended toward the moody and melodramatic but were honest and loyal always, had vowed I would come to accept my lot, and, of course, I have. After years of resentment, what I care most about now is the work itself.

I begin writing at midnight, and do not stop, not even for a drink of water, until five. Twice, I nearly forgot myself and, caught up in a creative whirlwind, risked discovery by the other members of the household: I kept on at the computer until noon, so involved in my story that I didn't realize I had left drops of my own blood on the keyboard. I always make certain to conform to the style our author claims as her own, although, unlike my predecessors, I shy away from the moral issues of loyalty and obedience. I'm more straightforward, more story-driven, and I'm careful to check for too many references to swimming and running, activities I no longer have time for. Our author, on the other hand, often begins her day at the pool or the track. In the past, she would sit down to check spelling and grammar—after breakfast and the newspaper—complaining all the while, but now there is a software program for that, and frankly it's a relief to find that she's picked up an interest in sports. At least it gives her something to do.

Although I now see that our arrangement suits me, the secrecy has taken a toll. I'm guarded even with those to whom I'm closest. I gulp my food without chewing; I tend to pace. I worry that if we're exposed I will be banished to a kennel far out in the countryside, a place so rustic that my keepers will bring me only fruit when I howl for my Macintosh.

Recently, I feared that our author had been even more careless than usual. Without bothering to consult me, she has brought in a Polish Owczarek Nizinny, an ancient herding breed known for being independent. Already, this young herder is planning a novel—perhaps even a trilogy—about sheep and tennis balls, her primary interests. But now I see that with the proper training our little apprentice will come to understand the adjustments we must make for the sake of our work. All she needs to do is grace her characters with human names and form, to merely think of a tennis ball as a metaphor for redemption, a sort of rolling Holy Grail. No one will be the wiser then. As long as our author keeps her mouth shut.

Maureen Howard

a/k/a and l

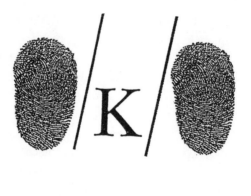

*H*oward, Maureen, nee Kearns, now Probst. All these names all my fault. But not being born. *Also known as* seems criminal though it is merely legal and the check, my friend, is good though not in the male. A surname for her name? It's only personal, personal history while the public is all too unrecognizable—a byline, name on a spine, tagged at a literary nonevent. Why are we here? Such a question—catechismal. She was raised Catholic. No, *here*. Oh, that Howard, that Maureen at the event. Because I did not know enough to stay home. Home is where her heart is and her work. I like a cliché when given a turn in its plot, and like sitting the long lone nameless hours, a woman with her work basket, the needles and threads a/k/a words. I am fond of calendars, astronomy, impersonal history, the delectable small facts as well as the sweeping time line that I clutch at the end for dear life.

Unknown to despair, Miss Stein, whom Howard admires, talked and talked and expired in her bed; while Mrs. Woolf, whom I love, weighed the stones for her pockets, choosing her baptismal death. Both women a/k/a s —their selves and their others. It is the other that Howard honors in these women, though she dare not see it in herself. If on some pages I have known the answer, it is because she made it up.

It is no great secret that she has committed novels and is obsessed with the unwriting, picking out the threads to find the honest story, which appears, then disappears the moment it is said. William James believed that for those who confessed, sham was over and realities begun. A simple view in my undivided opinion for truth and fancy, intertwined in their design, appear as fractals, immeasurable as grace; impossible as the aerial act that Howard a/k/a Little Mary, Mo, Mimi, Mom attempts in high-flown stories with the knowledge that she is simply Maureen, grounded in her ephemeral writing life.

Evan Hunter

Me and Ed

I don't like to examine the process of writing too closely because I'm afraid I'll somehow jinx it. But a little while ago, I discovered something about me and Ed that somewhat startled me. I'm referring to Ed McBain, of course, the fellow who writes the crime novels. I first began using his name when I was very young. The older and much wiser men then guiding my career felt that if it became known Evan Hunter was also writing *mysteries,* I would be drummed out of the Fraternal Order of Serious Writers.

They were right, of course.

I understand now why John P. Marquand disowned his enormously popular "Mr. Moto" series, and why Graham Greene insisted on calling his *non*serious novels "entertainments." My mentors could not have imagined, however, that *crime* writers would believe Evan Hunter was slumming and I would eventually become a writer with a foot in either camp and a true home in neither. But that has nothing to do with the recent discovery I made about me and Ed and the writing each of us continues to do under separate bylines.

In 1956, two years after *The Blackboard Jungle,* I published two novels within months of each other. One was by Evan

Hunter, and it was titled *Second Ending.* The other was by Ed McBain, and it was titled *Cop Hater.* The Hunter novel was a serious study of drug addiction; my closest friend had been a heroin addict who died not from an overdose but from tetanus. The McBain novel was a simple Smoke Screen mystery. Both were well reviewed. Both sold only modestly well. Only one of them is still in print. Guess which?

But the interesting thing about that first 87th Precinct novel was not that it broke any new ground—which I feel it did, by the way—but that it was so similar in style and content to *The Blackboard Jungle.* Both novels dealt with serious urban problems: education and crime. Both were set in a sprawling metropolis: New York in the Hunter novel, a fictitious Isola in the McBain. In each, the action centered on a public building: a school and a police station. Within these larger structures, the setting focused on hangouts where the characters met to comment on the action: the teachers' lunchroom and the detective squadroom. In each novel, the character breakdown was patterned on a big-city racial and religious mix. In each, the grimness of the plot was offset by a dark humor.

On the other hand, *Second Ending,* the almost prophetically titled Hunter novel, was virtually humorless. It tried so veddy veddy hard to be "serious," don't you know, that it forgot all the craft I'd learned in the years preceding publication of *The Blackboard Jungle.* This would continue to be the case in subsequent years. As Hunter, I kept searching for Hunter, experimenting with different styles in each novel, making myself impossible to categorize, for the most part forgetting humor except when I was writing a deliberately "comic" novel labeled as such. At the same time, the McBain style remained essentially unchanged. That is to say, it was the style *Hunter* had used in *The Blackboard Jungle,* a straightforward, dead-serious prose, leavened with humor.

The discovery I made . . .

And I truly hope this *doesn't* jinx what I write from now on . . .

Though I don't think it will because I've just finished a new "serious" novel and I'm happy to say it's funny and suspenseful as well . . .

The discovery I made is that Ed McBain is the *true* lineal descendant of Evan Hunter, and not the bastard progeny I'd assumed he was all along.

Ed, I'm home.

Take my hand.

Diane Johnson

Diane Johnson and I

*J*ohnson. That is not her name, and it isn't my name, just a name picked up from an early husband. She was too timid —should I say too weak in character—to resist it, didn't want to hurt the feelings of the husband and the editor. The idea of the editor was that her real name was too actressy for a serious writer.

Still, she is more used to being Diane Johnson than I am. I am Dinny, Mom, Mrs. or Professor Murray—an array of names not Diane Johnson, though over the years I have learned to answer to her name, too.

Who is she when she is alone? I think, when she is alone, writing, she is Diane Lain (her real name), or Dinny Lain, the nickname we both started out with. The too-actressy names. It is I who have taken on the personas that go with the new names. Wreathed in pseudonyms, I do my marketing, talk to the plumber, teach the class. I am more brisk, cheerful and thoughtless than she. She is mild, unassertive, solitary.

I think we tended at first to keep her in her place for fear she would get uppity and oppress the children with the idea of her Work; but now she is altogether too diffident (or is it lazy?). My knitting projects—sewing, recipes and notes to write—

crowd out her hesitant paragraphs scribbled on envelopes. She can't find them; she hesitates to demand more space for them. She doesn't have a room of her own. Poor wretch! If I were in charge of her, I would try to give her some backbone.

From day to busy day I hurry around, without thoughts, saving them for her. So I wish she had better thinking and working habits. She could shape my thoughts more regularly. If she were in my charge I would try to inspirit her, and tell her it is her duty to do her writing work. That is how I would change her, if she were in my charge.

And if I were in *her* charge, she would instill habits in me, who am without them and must start each day figuring things out all over from scratch.

Edward P. Jones

Disappearing

*N*ot many years ago, I became aware that EDvark p JOnes was across the Potomac River from me in Washington, where I had become a writer. A close friend called to say she had seen me about in my old neighborhoods with an Afroed woman on my arm. I was wearing an expensive, three-piece suit. I was beardless and without a moustache, the friend had said. With three small children. I paid her no mind, because none of that fit who I am across the river. But when she and others called many times after that to say they kept seeing me about, I went across the river and walked the neighborhoods for weeks. Finally, I saw him one spring evening on 10th Street and, without hesitating, he stepped up to me. "Edward, I'm EDvark," he said, shifting the youngest child to his other arm. "I looked for you and found you only in your work, your scarce work. Now you are in the flesh and it makes a difference." "At last, we have met the Edward," the woman with the Afro said with an accent I could not recognize. EDvark gave me his card: "EDvark p JOnes: writer-to-be." "We have lived across the ocean," the woman said, "where writing is not done. Where EDvark could not be EDvark, or even Edward." Soon enough, I left them and went back across the Potomac.

Ultimately, I remembered where I had first seen that name—thirty years before in junior high school. I had gotten my very first chance to use a typewriter and after several tries managed to write my name correctly on a lone piece of paper after many misspellings on other discarded pages. My name spelled correctly and perfectly looked like a miracle and I sensed then I would never be the same after seeing my name written down in cold, unflinching typescript: The wonder of the letters made me want to see my name that way again and again, eternally. I added a "by" above my name and it seemed even more perfect and my heart took flight. Without knowing it, I had signed on and was sailing off to an island of words and I would not return. I turned away from the desk for less than the blink of an eye and when I returned, someone had written beneath my name "by EDvark p JOnes," which was one of my misspellings on a discarded piece of paper.

Now, these days, a bearded and moustachioed EDvark is living in my apartment across the river. I did not give him a key or an invitation to stay and the Afroed woman and the children are gone. I see mostly shadow glimpses of EDvark. Perhaps he lives in the walls, in the computer. His card is taped to the bathroom mirror and magneted to the icebox. My work is now being returned as unsatisfactory, work I spent eternities on. "Is this the work of the Edward P. Jones I saw in such and such a book, in such and such a magazine?" they write when my work is returned. I call them and ask for a second chance, and in cases where I do get another chance, the work is still returned, addressed to me, but I note changes I know I did not make. I leave messages about for EDvark to leave my stuff, my work, alone. I am beginning to doubt the talent the people in the island of words told me I had. The last straw was yesterday—an acceptance came in his name: "This is the old Edward I've known for so long," the note said. "Why are you spelling your name differently now? Is it the beginning of something new?"

Ward Just

Just and unJust

*H*e suspects they hand him a cocktail hoping for a transfiguration, and that before their eyes he will become someone of consequence—an ambassador, a translator of German literature, a United States senator, a soldier of fortune, a beautiful and wanton artist, even. God knows he's trying to look the part, to live up to the expectations he assumes they have; so he wears a regimental tie and a tweed jacket of a color not seen since the Kennedy Administration (a jibe from a recent interview that he tracked like a professional hunter, searching for the spoor of candor).

He believes they are listening for the rhythms he knows are his trademark, clipped sentences, inventories of things. And perhaps, speaking the trademark lingo, he can wing them away to one of his many exotic locations, Berlin, Washington, Paris, Peru, not forgetting the press tent at Danang and a golf club in Winnetka. Goodness, there's excitement aplenty in these places on the printed page, despair, vainglory, vulgarity, betrayal, anarchy, parricide, happiness beyond measure.

But the truth is, they are not waiting for anything. They hope for nothing, want nothing, expect nothing. They have no idea who he is, though they've heard a rumor or two about me.

Poor Just, he believes they're waiting for a smart remark, something to remember him by. So he fires a salvo, anything to put them off stride.

The gin's good.

Hasn't there been a lot of rain lately?

Not that I'm bored. Don't *you* love Martha's Vineyard in December?

On Sunday, I'll be watching the golf on television.

The Skins Game, thirty large a hole. I'm rooting for Arnie.

His swing's gone to hell. But he's got heart.

And all the time he's talking, I'm listening, bored out of my wits. The Just and the unJust inhabiting the same body, so close you can't pry us apart, but we are not friends. He speaks, I edit. He plays, I work. He is famously convivial, I am a recluse. And at the end of the evening, when I'm exhausted and yearning for bed, knowing there's an assignment to complete, he stays on, anything to keep me in the closet a little longer. And when the inevitable question comes, he answers it with aplomb, holding out his glass—

Don't mind if I do.

Ivan Klíma

Translated from the Czech by Paul Wilson

Klíma and I

I can't tell you much about Klíma, and what I do know is mostly secondhand—from a vast array of facts and opinions that I can neither confirm nor deny. I have also read high praise of him in foreign magazines and newspapers, which I explain thus: First, they don't really know him, and second, my own limited knowledge of languages means that I may occasionally take seriously something that might have been tongue-in-cheek. Friends tell me he works hard and likes to write. That is possible. I tend to work hard only occasionally, and whenever I sit down to face a sheet of paper or my computer screen, I can always come up with at least ten things I'd rather be doing. I'd rather cook a three-course meal than write a three-line letter. Poor Klíma has to write at least twenty letters a week. If it were me, I'd rather go off to a cave and live a hermit's life.

They say Klíma enjoys making public appearances, that he's immune to stage fright, and that women claim he's a Don Juan and has a way with them, although that's the kind of rumor spread by people who've never seen him and know him only from what's been randomly published or translated somewhere. For my part, I tend to be shy and don't have much of a way with women at all. It takes a great deal of effort for me to screw up my courage and speak to women I like. Mostly I hope they will speak to me first, but understandably it has never happened, because they mistake me for Klíma the Don Juan, and wait for me to make the first move. Once a woman I knew only by sight but whom I found very attractive became tipsy at a party and told me she loved me. Unfortunately I didn't know her name and was too ashamed to ask, and I never saw her again.

Klíma and I of course share some of the same biographical data. Both of us were locked up by the Nazis during the war, but whereas I remember almost nothing of that time (I have both a terrible memory and a talent for forgetting unpleasant experiences), Klíma can improvise entire chapters on that theme in his novels. Also, both of us were in America in the early seventies but returned to live in occupied Czechoslovakia. They said Klíma did so because he was brave; I returned because I didn't have the courage to start all over again in a foreign country, and also because I'm an utterly conservative person who likes home best of all. Both Klíma and I are happily married and naturally we've spent our whole lives with one woman. We have two children and even some grandchildren. But there are millions of people like that in the world.

I could say a lot more about myself, but who would be interested? I'm not a very neat person; I don't like wearing ties and I'm not easily upset. What I don't write down I forget. I often run into people who claim to be acquaintances of mine, though I have the feeling I've never seen them before. Unfortunately this happens more and more all the time.

I like hunting for wild mushrooms, I play tennis and go for walks in the countryside, I read (nonfiction—I'm not very fond of pure literature and I'm surprised that people still read it, let alone write it). I also collect old maps and printed material, and artifacts of Scottish and Irish folklore.

Klíma has no time for any of that because he is hard at work in front of his computer from morning to night, writing. You ask me what I think of him. I don't want to hurt his feelings but the fact is I feel rather sorry for him. What can the poor fellow possibly get out of life?

Ed Koren

My Appendage

Elmore Leonard

What Elmore Leonard Does

*W*hat he does, he makes us do all the work, the people in his books. Puts us in scenes and says, "Go ahead and do something." No, first he thinks up names, takes forever to think up names like Bob and Jack, Jackie for a woman, the female lead. Or Frank. Years ago anyone named Frank in one of his books was a bad guy. So then he used Frank as the name of the good guy one time and this Frank wouldn't talk, refused to come out and become the kind of person Elmore wanted; so he changed his name to Jack after thinking of names for another few weeks and it felt so good you couldn't shut the guy up. I mean this Jack, not Elmore. So he names us and says, "Okay, start talking," and that's what we do. Sometimes, if a character has trouble expressing himself, he's demoted, is given less to do in the book, or, he might get shot. What can also happen, if a minor or even a no-name character shows he can talk, he can shove his way into the story and get a more important part. So, Elmore names us, gets us talking to each other, bumping heads or getting along okay and then, I don't know what happens to him. I think he takes off, leaves it up to us. There was a piece written about him one time in the *Village Voice* called "The Author Vanishes" and it's true.

Romulus Linney

On My Name

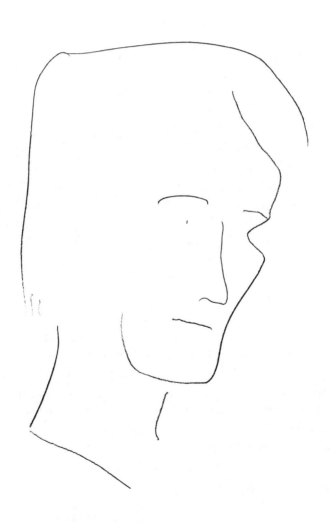

*R*omulus. Go through life thinking twice. With that kind of name you can get schizophrenic. It is preposterous to be named after the first Emperor of Rome. It is also Southern tradition to have such a name—I am the fourth Romulus—with a middle name equally bizarre: Zachariah. One name from the classics, one from the Bible, with the last, good plain Linney, from Wales. Romulus Zachariah Linney. How can anyone so named write—never mind publish—out of a self presented under so ludicrous a banner? How escape the inquiries about Remus? At sixty-three, I find its shadow was present while I tried most to avoid it, writing plays and novels about modest American characters in the Appalachian mountains but then turning around and doing the same about Frederick the Great, Lord Byron and Hermann Goering. Up one side, as my mountaineers say, and down the other.

Two selves, sliced apart by a name. Bill Linney, aspiring to modesty and virtue, Romulus Zachariah equally so to grandiosity and exaltation. Actor on a stage and recluse in an empty room. So my "authorial I" is riven and ambivalent, the mixed feelings it writes from dominant. And that, unmistakably, is me, seeking virtue in villainy and villainy in virtue, all at the same time, to be confronted with mystery in everything. That is truth to me and I seem to accept no other.

I've known people who thought their names misrepresented their true selves, but I can't be one of them. Whether it fit me when I was born or I lived my life to fit it—ambiguity right there—I don't know. But it does, finally, fit, and finally, the self I am, out of custom, absurdity and a life spent writing, is well named.

William Matthews

The Complaint

I don't complain that he has misrepresented me, for the impersonation is skillful. Slander is scarcely the issue: On balance, he has made me seem both a livelier and better person than I fear I am.

People who make the mistake that I am he expect an ironic skepticism, a bruised worldliness, and, maybe, like a caption you wouldn't have thought a picture needed until an exact one got supplied, an apt little tag phrase, maybe in Latin. He is, people say, witty, and also smart. I feel like a widower's bride being told of her brilliant predecessor, and I fill with formless murk.

The people who tell me these things while I stand stiffly mute are not the ones to whom I seem both a livelier and better person than I really am, needless to say.

People I've never met make that mistake, and why would I have met them? Who stands behind a podium and theatrically extracts his reading glasses from a nifty leather case, rocks back on his heels and unreels some genial patter, and then reads, in that cigarette-rasped old-friends voice of his, a poem which the hipper members of the audience applaud by making small, barely but firmly audible, all-vowel noises, like gerbil orgasms? Who travels to the Rockefeller Foundation's Study and Confer-

ence Center on Lake Como to write for a month under a cantile-
vered Tizio lamp, and then returns with droll instructions on
how to find the best *gelati* in Bellagio? Mr. Travel On Other People's Money, that's who. Mr. Leisure Of The Theory Class.

Well, I guess you can hear the resentment now. I'm the
emotional one, wit be damned, and he's broken my heart. It
wasn't always like this. In the beginning, I wallowed in his at-
tentions.

"Me?" I would think, fluttering at the mirror.

Then: "Me!"

Then, of course, I knew, or thought I knew, what he
wanted. But now? Material? He's not an "autobiographical"
writer. I often recognize my emotions, of course, in his poems.
But they're shorn of the exact details and private references that
made them mine. They have details and references he's made
up, but those could be anyone's. And anyone's are drab.

That's why I resent him. OK, I'm very emotional and easily
filled with formless murk, and sometimes I get weepy like this,
I'm sorry. Yes, thank you. He's glib, he files his tongue before he
brushes his teeth, and he's diligent as a dog. He hasn't called in
two days.

He looks like me, but happier.

I don't suppose this will matter to your investigation, but I
stole the phrase "formless murk" from a rejected draft of one of
his poems. "Stole" is perhaps the wrong word. He'd thrown it
away. I didn't have to uncrumple any paper. It was in plain view.
He owes me a lot.

What? That's not a hard question. Of course it's a domestic
dispute. After all, which of the persons I mentioned is missing?

Peter Mayle

....

Mayle and I

*H*e is an uncomfortable companion—a nag, a fretter, a seeker after work, a spoilsport. I am often content to pass my days in the garden or with a book. He isn't. He feels that I am wasting time that should be devoted to writing. I can enjoy a long morning in a café with no particular purpose, watching the casual drift of humanity on the sidewalk. He can't. He wants to observe, to take notes that will be tucked away for future polishing and turned into sentences.

This is irritating enough, although the passage of time has reduced the irritation to the level of a minor affliction, a distant murmur of activity in an otherwise placid mind. That side of him, no more than a subliminal buzz, can be endured, as one endures myopia, hangovers and other small inconveniences. But what is more serious, and sometimes quite disturbing, is his infuriating detachment.

You can't take him anywhere—at least, not with any confidence that he will forget himself sufficiently to enter into the spirit of the proceedings without assessing them for possible use. I am having dinner with friends, taking pleasure in the mild euphoria induced by good food and conversation. Not him. He is off to one side, watching our gradual slip from sobriety, his ear cocked to pick up the indiscretions that come from tongues made loose by wine.

And he is callous. I fall one day and break my wrist. Far from being sympathetic, he is angry. His only concern is that the accident and several days of acute pain will reduce the ration of words committed to paper.

He receives most news, good or bad, with an equal lack of involvement, as though it were nothing but grist, to be weighed and sifted to gauge its value. Joy or despair, disappointment or triumph, frustration or relief—it often seems to me that he regards them as raw material, rather than emotions.

Only occasionally is there a dent in his detachment, when he shows himself to be a sensitive little soul, easily bruised by unkind words. When criticized, he mopes. But oddly enough, he consistently disbelieves praise. I think he is by nature a pessimist.

I, on the other hand, am an optimist, always hopeful (or so I like to think) of finding redeeming features in the least promising of characters. Even him.

Being prone to idleness myself, I admire his diligence, his professional conscience and his ability to resist distraction. I admire his memory, which is prodigious, although highly selective. And I have to admit that he has a well-developed sense of the absurd, particularly where I am concerned. He refuses to take me seriously, and that is as it should be.

Above all, he enables me to avoid having to take part in the corporate merry-go-round, doing what my mother used to call honest work, surrounded by men in suits. For that, I am profoundly grateful.

I suppose I rather like him.

Leonard Michaels

Michaels Writing

I heard a writer say███████████████bout me. Now let's talk about my work." ███████████████m is endemic to the writer's life, and, if ███████████████another way.

Apparently, ███████████████ If we were susceptible ███████████████re could be no joke, but Ap███████████████ ██M and Apple. We lack supern███████████████ can █ven ta█k about our writ███████████████ Borges, in his essay on ███████████████ saving ██ isn't even a writer. ███████████████o is the writer. As ██o███████████████s the streets of Bue██ ██ an█ █ith h█████████ng charm, says: I am no███ ██ho █████ an█

Socrates w███████████████ Naturally, he did███████████████and a da███████ spirit, and was subject █████████o you mi█h█ s████ █ would at least keep a jo███ █ ███ocial life █████logue to the loneliness of a bla████ge███ud█ ██ █n ugly ██████eared the page as if it were ██ ██a█ Writin█ ██ seemed ████ ironical invitation to narc███

Once Socrates ██ ██invited █ d███ er part█ ██ ██ thon, the handsome, prize-win███████ ██nged██es. F█ ██ ██casion, Socrates, who alway████ ████ought s█████. H█ ██ ██id they were a show of respect fo█ ██ handsomeness o█ Agathon. █h█y were also a show of contempt, lo███ ██ the prize-wi████r who happen██d to be something of a dope. ███████ ██y made extremely famous by Plato in The Symposium, ended ██ Socrates trying to ██rsuade Aristophanes and Agathon th██ a ██ who writes comedies could also write tragedies. Arist██ ██es, ██ ██ been an amazingly wonderful talker during the ██arty, say the a █████ an attack on h█mself, for if Agathon █nd ██ were essentially iden████ ██ ██ wa█ █ dope. Arist██ ██ ██ off in the middle of the argument, which was hu██ ██ ██ jealous Socra█es since nobody remained for him to p█ ██ █ █he beauty queen.

██ ██ ousand years later ██when Montaigne grasped Socrates' █ing, he █nnihilated the wri██'s embarrassment by inventing the █ the most brilliant piece of █utzpa in western literature. It █ ██inues to be imitated until this very momen█, though hardly ever ver█ ██████. The entire matter of h█ essays, says Montaigne, is himself. F██ ██ ██more he say█ ██ ██ de him as much as he made it. Who

A joke among writers goes like this: "We've talked enough about me. Now let's talk about my work." It suggests that narcissism is endemic to the writer's life. If you deny it one way, you confess it another way.

I don't think the joke is too funny. It makes me squirm. If writers were still thought to be inspired, or susceptible to divine madness, there would be no such joke. It is supposed to make us laugh at our central anxiety, which is that the gods and the muses have fled. We have lost our ancient calling. Writing has come to resemble politics, or a sly kind of salesmanship. But people who don't write don't see it that way. They continue to ask writers strange questions like "Do you use a computer?" Maybe they think the instrument has magical power, or they believe writing is still haunted by gods. Not Apollo and Dionysus, but IBM and Apple. Of course the instrument makes no difference if writing lacks supernatural sanction.

To escape the spiritual desolation of narcissism, if nothing else, some writers imagine that their art is a high and mysterious endeavor, separate from ordinary life. Borges, for example, says he isn't even a writer. There is a second self, a spectral Borges, who is the writer, distinct from the plain fellow, the uninspired Borges who walks the streets of Buenos Aires. In effect, with self-alienating irony, Borges says: "I am not the writer who writes 'I am not the writer who writes,'" etc.

Socrates was the first to notice the writer's dilemma. It's known that he had a demon or tutelary spirit, and was subject to trancelike states, so you might suppose he would be a writer. But he refused to pick up the pen. He much preferred the pleasures of social life and dialogue to the loneliness of a blank page. Indeed, he feared the page as an invitation to narcissism.

About two thousand years later, Montaigne, who grasped Socrates' meaning profoundly, annihilated the writer's dilemma by inventing the essay. An amazing achievement. Its entire matter was the man himself turned into language, shaped by the psychological principles of his being or his soul. The ideas in Montaigne's essays, even when borrowed from others, became *his* ideas in the way he understood them and put them. He said if you want to know about Montaigne, read his book, for his book made Montaigne as much as he made it. His book is a living self, a life, or a human freedom unanticipated and unconstrained by a preexisting form. He said he wrote it for his beloved family. They could remember him by virtue of his book, as if he were still in the room, still talking, the familiar man. Today, learned critics struggle to define the essay, rather as if its source, family life, has been largely forgotten, or else remembered only as an abyss of secret debauchery out of which we crawled toward adulthood.

Recently, Michel Foucault, an admirer of Borges, reviewed the ancient dilemma of writers with a sort of hysterical frivolity. There might be writers—he was one himself—but he said there are no "authors." Nobody inspired, original, authentic. Our books are instances of discourse, cast up in the endless babbling of the race. Foucault isn't altogether wrong, but, as in the joke about a pretentious man, one thinks: "Look who is no author."

Of the four, I find Montaigne sympatico and most pertinent

to me, or what I might call the experience of myself as a writer. Without forgetting about my occasional back trouble, sleepless nights, and gruesome depressions, it is the spiritual aspect of writing that I see in the way Montaigne moves amid ideas and passions. He also reminds me of Frank, my girlfriend's cat, who glides amid the furniture of our house, sniffing, rubbing, scratching. Frank makes these investigative essays every day, drawn to some things more than others. Rubbing against the leg of a chair, Frank makes it his own by experiencing it. Not only the chair, but also himself by contrast, the form of life he is. For me, this is not only like Montaigne, but much like writing.

I notice a deer standing in my garden, surprised, struck rigid with horror, staring at me. I don't know what the deer sees, but I'm sure that I exist for him absolutely, a finished thing, as I could never exist for myself. Then I feel the deer's own horror when I see a human self materialized, as in body builders or fashion models, or others who lust for the condition of things. I see it in writers who make themselves into appearances, reading aloud from their work. Now and then, I confess, I do that too, but it's only for a little money and to hear people laugh.

The telephone rings. "Hello," I say. The word *Hello* comes first, and then, an instant behind the word, I arrive. After I put down the telephone, I persist in the psychological inertia of conversation, a mental voice like the vapor trail of a jet plane, the silent record of sound. It reminds me of the difference between what is in my head and what appears on the page when I write.

"Writing," says Freud, "is the record of an absent person," but every word is the record of absent persons. In my case, they are mainly English and Yiddish speakers who preceded me and died. When I write, I join a silent conversation.

James A. Michener

Michener and I

et's get one thing straight. I am the real James Michener. But that doesn't get us very far, because Michener is not my real name. Nobody knows what it is, was or should be. I was a foundling with no track record, so I could be Hindu, part African American, a Jew, a Catholic or a Norwegian. I have to be careful about saying anything bad about any group because I might belong to it.

The Micheners who took me under their benevolent wing were an amazing tribe of Quakers who came over with William Penn in the late 1600s. In the first version of our family history the author said truthfully: "They were indentured servants." Everyone raised the devil about that and promptly in the second printing we were "Sturdy English yeomen advisors to William Penn." In the next edition Penn will be found coming over with us.

The fact that there is no clear record as to who I am has made it inviting for others to invent a family history for me, and to establish fanciful relationships with me. The real Micheners were a prolific lot, with my home county containing several James A's. They never gave me any trouble.

But others, widely scattered, have. One, who went to my

college, organized a spurious trip to the South Pacific on a cruise liner, promising that a James A. would accompany and lead the group. He collected funds and drew the attention of the legal authorities. Another sashayed through the bazaars of Asia making huge purchases and signing for them in my name. In due course he, too, was arrested. Now numerous supposed relatives are making sounds as if they intend to challenge my will, whenever it is probated.

But there is also a James A. in northern Virginia who is a most delightful man. Same age as me, same handwriting, he's a Marine colonel and our association has been a warm and rewarding one.

But now we reach another James A. Michener who gives me deep trouble. Through the years sensible critics and commentators have claimed that since I have written so many books on such a wide variety of subjects, I simply must have a secret staff who do the research. And, say many of the believers, "they actually write the books and Michener signs them as if they were his own work." A mystical James A. is in charge of this operation and the canard has become so widespread and so persuasive that I have come to believe it.

I see myself as the shell of a man who behaves himself and presents an amiable face to the public, while the real Michener and his staff of twenty labor in some shadowy hall, writing the books and bringing the finished manuscripts to me to sign. It's been a strange symbiosis, this fruitful working of these two James A's.

The accusations would distress me had I not known Irving Berlin in his later years. Few people realize that the last public song he wrote was "Sayonara" in the exciting days when he and Josh Logan and I were planning a musical version of that book. When I told him about my struggle with the various Micheners he said: "Don't worry. All my professional life I've been plagued by the rumor that I don't write my own songs. They're all written by a meek little man I keep in a private room and pay twenty-eight dollars a week. It's always twenty-eight bucks." He paused, then said: "The problem is to find the right little man. When you find someone who can write your books, be generous with him. Give him twenty-nine a week."

I haven't found the right man and remain Michener the schizoid. I don't know who I am, but this leaves me free to imagine myself as practically anyone, and that's not a bad skill for a writer to have.

Arthur Miller

Arthur Miller

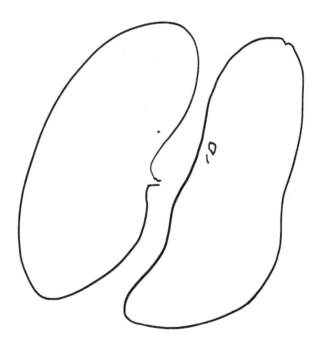

Rumor

*L*ook who thinks he is Updike! And Milosz! Not to speak of Borges! Nobody is these actual people, of course. Why pretend? Merely are they names of attitudes which certain people with the same names have managed to attach themselves to. Who is Homer? Who is Shakespeare? Nobody. And does it matter? Supposing there was discovered in some hidden tomb pages of writing describing one "Homer," a widely traveled poet who was last seen disappearing into an Aegean whirlpool? Supposing even that he was notorious for having returned from a long poem-selling trip to discover that his wife was living with eleven suitors who were hanging around his house hoping she would give in; and that in a temper he had slain them all, and that for this he was famous all over the islands? How would this change "The Odyssey"?

For one thing, people could then go around saying "The Odyssey" is "nothing but" his autobiography, so you don't have to read it, just as you had always hoped you wouldn't have to. Or, on the other hand, knowing it was "nothing but his own life disguised," you might start reading "The Odyssey" after avoiding it since high school. But would you be reading it for the right reasons? Or is there such a thing as the right reason to read a book?

I know Arthur Miller but not "Arthur Miller" or *Arthur Miller* or "Miller." About twenty-five years ago the Romanian government banned all "Miller" plays as pornographic. Privately I was very pleased, having admired Henry Miller's work for a long time. Two theaters were in the midst of producing plays of mine and were forced to cancel them. Did this make me—slightly—Henry Miller? Or him—slightly—Arthur Miller? Or change Willy Loman into a brassiere salesman famous for his eagerness to supervise a proper fit for his merchandise? (I'm sure the Romanian censor must have found *something* suggestive in my plays.)

As with some others who are mistaken for the names they bear, the mention of "Miller" in the public press causes an instantaneous flight reaction in me, as though an accusation has been made which has some truth in it. If the name is accompanied by praise I cautiously get back into position, standing beneath the name but without any firm conviction that it and I are one and the same. If the name is condemned I tend to feel a closer identification, of course, but never a complete one lest I cut off my escape route, the escape to "myself."

Last year a cab driver looked into his rearview mirror and said, "You look like Arthur Miller, but I know you're not." I asked him how he knew I wasn't. "You look halfway decent," he said. I could only agree.

A book, a poem, a play—they start as fantasms but they end up as *things*, like a box of crackers or an automobile tire. Whoever buys them owns them. The name on the jacket or poster is finally like "Nabisco," "Goodyear," a spoonful of associations with this or that quality of reassurance or questionable value.

So go ahead and make whatever you like of this. It's yours.

Czeslaw Milosz

My Double

A scrupulous conscience is not the best kind of conscience. It is inclined to self-torture, with valid reasons or not. That is why the existence of Milosz the writer is for me a constant annoyance. I do not even remember how his works have been written. His life—as it may be imagined by his readers—has very little to do with my life. Precisely because of his pretending he is me, my scrupulous conscience rebels. It invokes all the days and months of doubt, despair, blind groping, all my unconfessed shames, and asks: Where do you see them in Milosz? He professes to write truth but omits so much that in both his poetry and prose he reminds me of somebody jumping from one ice floe to another and pretending there is no black water between. He argues that the law of form allows a limited amount of reality only, while I would like to provide every sentence of his with a commentary which, I concede, probably would be an exercise in self-pity.

When he received the Nobel Prize, he dragged me everywhere, for ceremonies and banquets, and I was sitting there like a dummy with the tag of his name, puzzled and uneasy. Even worse, when I was greeted in Poland as a national bard coming home, I tried hard not to laugh, for the transformation of a hermetic poet into a football star was grotesque, and yet I was caught in a role somehow prepared for me in his script.

It is true that many times, in interviews, in conversations about him, I have made attempts to mark my distance. I undermined his stanzas full of anger at human crimes by bringing forth my own dirt and denounced his words of faith as his self-defense against my skepticism. But those were paltry remedies unable to break our cohabitation in one person.

There has been also a dream of taking his place and appearing as I really am. It visited me after the publication of every new book of his and after many books it is as strong as ever, but now I see it is too late.

Mary Morris

My Persona and Me

*P*eople who read my books say, "I feel as if I know you." They write me letters or come to readings to hear me talk. Of course they know nothing, I want to reply, but I am too polite. You are so courageous, they tell me. You do things I never could. How can I tell them that I am a coward, that I hate to take risks? That I dread heights, waterfalls, rats, airplanes, cars careening in the dark night, drunken drivers, food I've never tasted, sleeping on the floor?

They want to know if everything is true. Am I in touch with Lupe? Did I marry the photographer? I tell them that Lupe is a real person with whom I have sadly lost touch. But the photographer is a fictive character in a novel so it would be difficult to marry him.

I write fiction and nonfiction. About journeys, inner and outer. I tell an audience that there is much truth in my fiction, much invention in my nonfiction. A restless buzzing can be heard. The audience isn't comfortable with the response. I am a storyteller. I make things up. All the time. But they do not believe me. They do not want to believe. Your mother didn't abandon you when you were a child? There wasn't a ghost in the hills that protected you outside San Miguel?

I try to explain before the questioning looks. My life has been filled with abandoning mothers, ghosts, sisters who disappear, totemic animals and men I can't quite trust, drowning boys and barracuda who snap at my heels, brothers who are damaged goods, wars fought in distant lands, gunrunners and guerrillas, women who take me in, broken-down buses, childhood fears, houses in snowstorms, my own house where I lived as a girl, dreams. Endless dreams of railroads and flying. Me swimming through the air so that I believe upon waking that I actually did swim.

How can I answer the question of what really happened? People say you are so brave. Do I tell them that I am shy and retiring? That I never really take a risk? They think I am a nice person, fun to be with, who can tell good jokes before a crowd. Do I say I am happiest when left alone, that I love the quiet of an empty house, a cat clawing softly at the back screen, the wind through the oak tree? I screen my calls. Sometimes I don't answer my mail. I have long been drawn to cocoons, down comforters, tiny compartments to myself on trains.

Eventually they all ask the same question. But you were always alone, weren't you? You really were alone. I do not disappoint them here. Yes, I say, and for once I am not lying. I was always alone.

Thylias Moss

My Better Half

*I*t so happens that Thylias the writer is the better half of this marriage if talking dollars and sense, dominant versus recessive, fifteen minutes of fame, and number of listings in *Books in Print*. Properly, I defer to her achievement: She is the one certain of life though hers is papery, and certain that words are the means to all ends; she is the one whose doubts, if any, are insignificant, and don't threaten her ideologies that she will take to any forum, accepting honoraria for the visits where not much is required of her, just the reiteration of her writings. For these occasions, I lend her my physiological ability to produce sound; her voice is merely the articulate manipulation of thoughts. An audience would not be much satisfied with an exhibition of her thinking which, though active, is not memorable to watch. So while I contribute only anatomy's menial service, she realizes the difficulty she'd have proving hers the greater contribution, since she would need me to assert that proof, and some words I refuse to type for her, claiming carpal tunnel syndrome. There is necessary fraud involved. There would be nothing universal or personal without deceptions.

Her certainty of much that I question makes our debates useful; I'd like to win one. Since I can't explain her existence, she doesn't feel subject to boundaries, physics, or my guilt. Her sympathies are with the inexplicable, the death-defying, cold fusion. Having the exemption of angels, she doesn't need, as I would, to allow the possibility of regret to censor her publications; she says anything. If she persists, there won't be any secrets, none of the mysteries she reveres and exposes in the most unsavory places—tabloid news shows, sports, shopping malls, motels, music videos, the Psychic Friends Network, Sumo suits, "The Birth of a Nation." If problems arise, they're mine. I'm the one feeling mortality's pinches; I can be caged and harassed while she remains free to write, deriving at least that strange pleasure from anything.

The distance between us widens as she becomes something I can't be, someone I struggle to emulate, moving while I stand still, wondering by now why she married me, thinking about leaving, so I offer the seduction of details of my childhood that she can use for poems. See, I think to myself, she doesn't want you only for your body, those vibrating vocal cords, those agile fingers. Predictably, she seizes any thoughts I have, for there is no way to conceal them from her; she's swift, enterprising, compelled, and limited to that one duty of word-mongering. She knows she is better at saying anything I might have to say.

These began as my thoughts, but she, the articulate one, is more likely their arranger. She is hungry for ideas and it's my responsibility to feed her since she is more mine than I am hers, the way it always is with offspring. Who should get possession of this should we separate? The reader; of course, the reader. She has much to say about that, but my carpal tunnel syndrome is flaring up and changing the subject to inconvenience, the only subject, really.

Joyce Carol Oates

"JCO" and I

"JCO"

*I*t is a fact that, to that other, nothing ever happens. I, a mortal woman, move through my life with the excited interest of a swimmer in uncharted waters—my predilections are few, but intense—while she, the other, is a mere shadow, a blur, a figure glimpsed in the corner of the eye. Rumors of "JCO" come to me thirdhand and usually unrecognizable, arguing, absurdly, for her historical existence. But while *writing* exists, *writers* do not—as all writers know. It's true, I see her photograph—*my* "likeness"—yet it is rarely the same "likeness" from photograph to photograph, and the expression is usually one of faint bewilderment. *I acknowledge that I share a name and a face with "JCO,"* this expression suggests, *but this is a mere convenience. Please don't be deceived!*

"JCO" is not a person, nor even a personality, but a process that has resulted in a sequence of texts. Some of the texts are retained in my (our) memory, but some have bleached out, like pages of print left too long in the sun. Many of the texts have been translated into foreign languages, which is to say into texts at another remove from the primary—sometimes even the author's name, on the dust jacket of one of these texts, is unrecognizable by the author. I, on the contrary, am fated to be "real"—"physical"—"corporeal"—to "exist in Time." I continue to age year by year, if not hour by hour, while "JCO," the other, remains no fixed age—in spiritual essence, perhaps, forever poised between the fever of idealism and the chill of cynicism, a precocious eighteen years old. Yet, can a process be said to have an age? an impulse, a strategy, an obsessive tracery, like planetary orbits to which planets, "real" planets, must conform?

No one wants to believe this obvious truth: The "artist" can inhabit any individual, for the individual is irrelevant to "art." (And what is "art"? A firestorm rushing through Time, arising from no visible source and conforming to no principles of logic or causality.) "JCO" occasionally mines, and distorts, my personal history; but only because the history is close at hand, and then only when some idiosyncrasy about it suits her design, or some curious element of the symbolic. If you, a friend of mine, should appear in her work, have no fear—you won't recognize yourself, any more than I would recognize you.

It would be misleading to describe our relationship as hostile in any emotional sense, for she, being bodiless, having no existence, has no emotions: We are more helpfully defined as diamagnetic, the one repulsing the other as magnetic poles repulse each other, so that "JCO" eclipses me, or, and this is less frequent, I eclipse "JCO," depending upon the strength of my will.

If one or the other of us must be sacrificed, it has always been me.

And so my life continues through the decades . . . not connected in the slightest with that conspicuous other with whom, by accident, I share a name and a likeness. The fact seems self-evident that I was but the door through which she entered—"it" entered—but any door would have done as well. Does it matter which entrance you use to enter a walled garden? Once you're inside and have closed the door?

For once, not she but I am writing these pages. Or so I believe.

Edna O'Brien

Who Is Writing This

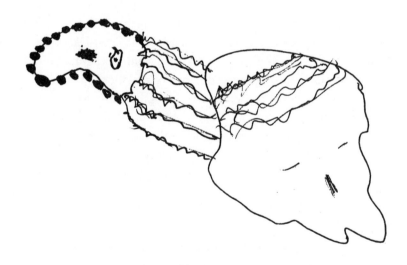

*T*he other me, who did not mean to drown herself, went under the sea and remained there for a long time. Eventually she surfaced near Japan and people gave her gifts but she had been so long under the sea she did not recognize what they were. She is a sly one. Mostly at night we commune. Night. Harbinger of dream and nightmare and bearer of omens which defy the music of words. In the morning the fear of her going is very real and very alarming. It can make one tremble. Not that she cares. She is the muse. I am the messenger. At given times she presides so that a word or a whole constellation of words are committed to paper. Her going like her coming is a fluke. I sometimes think I would sacrifice all other attachments to keep her and equally I wish that she had never come at all, because to be so beholden and so dependent is itself a little unnerving. She says Write whereas I say Live. The trouble is I do not know how to live whereas she knows how to write. She has more daring and more madness and surprisingly more sanity. She does not need people; I do. She is free but I am a prisoner. She can write about the mayhem of life without being overwhelmed by it. Being immaterial she will not request to be buried anywhere, whereas I have asked to lie next to my forebears whom I have spent my whole life running away from. Is she the spirit of another, a dead one perhaps. Moreover, does she intend to accompany me on the last outbound journey. To have to go on writing after death—what a terror. I don't know why I am so afraid of her. Maybe she is the Mother of all that is.

Cynthia Ozick

The Break

I write these words at least a decade after the terrifying operation that separated us. Unfortunately, no then-current anesthesia, and no then-accessible surgical technique, was potent enough to suppress consciousness of the knife as it made its critical blood-slice through the area of our two warring psyches. It is the usual case in medicine that twins joined at birth are severed within the first months of life. Given the intransigence of my partner (who until this moment remains recalcitrant and continues to wish to convert me to her loathesome outlook), I had to wait many years until I could obtain her graceless and notoriously rancorous consent to our divergence.

The truth is I have not spoken to her since the day we were wheeled, side by side as usual, on the same stretcher, into the operating room. Afterward it was at once observed (especially by me) that the surgery had not altered her character in any respect, and I felt triumphantly justified in having dragged her into it. I had done her no injury—she was as intractable as ever. As for myself, I was freed from her proximity and her influence. The physical break was of course the end, not the beginning, of our rupture; psychologically, I had broken with her a long time ago. I disliked her then, and though shut of her daily presence and unavoidable attachment, I dislike her even now. Any hint or symptom of her discourages me; I have always avoided reading her. Her style is clotted, parenthetical, self-indulgent, long-winded, periphrastic, in every way excessive—hard going altogether. One day it came to me: Why bother to keep up this fruitless connection? We have nothing in common, she and I. Not even a name. Since our earliest school years she has masqueraded as Cynthia, a Latin fancifulness entirely foreign to me. To my intimates I am Shoshana, the name given me at birth: Hebrew for Lily (anciently mistransliterated as Susanna).

To begin with, I am honest; she is not. Or, to spare her a moral lecture (but why should I? what has she ever spared *me*?), let me put it that she is a fantasist and I am not. Never mind that her own term for her condition is, not surprisingly, realism. It is precisely her "realism" that I hate. It is precisely her "facts" that I despise.

Her facts are not my facts. For instance, you will never catch me lying about my age, which is somewhere between seventeen and twenty-two. She, on the other hand, claims to be over sixty. A preposterous declaration, to be sure—but see how she gets herself up to look the part! She is all dye, putty, greasepaint. She resembles nothing so much as Gravel Gertie in the old Dick Tracy strip. There she is, done up as a white-haired, dewlapped, thick-waisted, thick-lensed hag, seriously myopic. A phenomenal fake. (Except for the nearsightedness, which, to be charitable, I don't hold against her, being seriously myopic myself.)

Aging is certainly not her only pretense. She imagines herself to be predictable; fixed; irrecoverable. She reflects frequently—tediously—on the trajectory of her life, and supposes that its arc and direction are immutable. What she has done she has done. She believes she no longer has decades to squander. I know better than to subscribe to such fatalism. Here the radical difference in our ages (which began to prove itself out at the moment of surgery) is probably crucial. It is her understanding that she is right to accept her status. She is little known or not known at all, relegated to marginality, absent from the authoritative anthologies that dictate which writers matter.

She knows she does not matter. She argues that she has been in rooms with the famous and felt the humiliation of her lesserness, her invisibility, her lack of writerly weight or topical cachet. In gilded chambers she has seen journalists and cultural consuls cluster around and trail after the stars; at conferences she has been shunted away by the bureaucratic valets of the stars. She is aware that she has not written enough. She is certainly not read. She sees with a perilous clarity that she will not survive even as "minor."

I will have none of this. There was a time—a tenuous membrane still hung between us, a remnant of sentiment or nostalgia on my part—when she was fanatically driven to coerce me into a similar view of myself. The blessed surgery, thank God, put an end to all that. My own ambition is fresh and intact. I can gaze at her fearfulness, her bloodless perfectionism and the secret crisis of confidence that dogs it, without a drop of concern. You may ask, Why are you so pitiless? Don't I know (I know to the lees) her indiscipline, her long periods of catatonic paralysis, her idleness, her sleepiness? Again you ask, Do you never pity her? Never. Hasn't she enough self-pity for the two of us? It is not that I am any more confident or less fearful; here I am, standing at the threshold still, untried, a thousand times more diffident, tremulous, shy. My heart is vulnerable to the world's distaste and dismissiveness. But oh, the difference between us! I have the power to scheme and to construct—a power that time has eroded in her, a power that she regards as superseded, useless. Null and void. Whatever shreds remain of her own ambitiousness embarrass her now. She is resigned to her failures. She is shamed by them. To be old and unachieved: ah.

Yes, ah! Ah! This diminution of hunger in her disgusts me;

I detest it. She is a scandal of sorts, a superannuated mourner; her Promethean wounds (but perhaps they are only Procrustean?) leak on her bed when she wakes, on the pavement when she walks. She considers herself no more than an ant in an anthill. I have heard her say of the round earth, viewed on films sent back from this or that space shuttle, that Isaiah and Shakespeare are droplets molten into that tiny ball, and as given to evaporation as the pointlessly rotating ball itself. Good God, what have I to do with any of that? I would not trade places with her for all the china in Teaneck.

Look, there is so much ahead! Forms of undiminished luminescence: specifically, novels. A whole row of novels. All right, let her protest if it pleases her—when *she* set out, the written word was revered; reputations were rooted in the literariness of poets, novelists. Stories are electronic nowadays, and turn up in pictures: the victory, technologically upgraded, of the comic book. The writer is at last delectably alone, dependent on no acclaim. It is all for the sake of the making, the finding, the doing: the *Ding-an-Sich*. The wild *interestingness* of it! I will be a novelist yet! I feel myself becoming a voluptuary of human nature, a devourer, a spewer, a seer, an ironist. A hermit-toiler. I dream of nights without sleep.

She, like so many of her generation, once sought work and recognition. Perhaps she labored for the sake of fame, who knows? Five or six of her contemporaries, no more, accomplished that ubiquitous desire. But here in the gyre of my eighteenth year, my goatish and unbridled twentieth, my muscular and intemperate and gluttonous prime, it is fruitfulness I am after: despite the unwantedness of it—and especially despite *her*—I mean to begin a life of novel-writing. A jagged heap of interferences beclouds the year ahead, but what do I care? I have decades to squander.

As for her: I deny her, I denounce her, I let her go. Whining, wizened, hoary fake, with her cowardice, her fake name!

Darryl Pinckney

Smokescreen

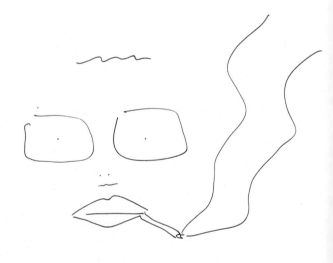

Darryl Pinckney

*W*hen I was starting out I was often reminded by teachers and editors that black people didn't read, the implication being that white people did and the most honorable thing I could do would be to become a translator of experience, a guide to feelings on the other side of town, because when a black person found his or her vocation as a writer the subject matter was taken for granted.

I wasted a lot of time questioning the notion that the autobiographical tradition since the slave narratives was a heavy chain from which there was no escape, that the idiom available to me was foreordained, that the elements of identity could be numbered like the pieces of clothing that made up the day's costume, and that everything I wrote would have two contexts, would disclose some aspect of the black condition, no matter what, because it would be always a black man who was doing the writing. The only consolation is that I would have wasted the time anyway. I have since figured out that white people, that other abstraction, don't read either, that language, English at least, stops for no one, and that as subjects go this one has all the possibilities. Its limitations are really my own.

I spent most of my beginning years as a writer stitching

together essays about black writers, especially dead ones, and in this way constructed for myself a History of Black Literature class I never took in college. The nice thing was that writing those essays delivered me without fuss from my self-conscious-ness to the subject I was born with. These intermittent appear-ances also offered me the validation of seeing my name in print. They whispered to me about a future and then kindly went away. Nothing stuck around to embarrass me for too long. I was not too troubled that before I knew it there was the writing that was asked for, addressed to anyone, and the writing that was unasked for, addressed ostensibly only to the self. I knew who wrote the reviews, but I had no idea who that other writer was trying to be. I suspect he was already nostalgic for the days when audience was a matter of friends on campus who took ev-ery hectic production with patience and when all the risks were still far off.

I was not too troubled because I was young and black. I ran around in the smoky dark of my cultural moment pretending that I was merely an observer storing up scenes. I fell for it: thought there would be something to say and time enough to say it in. But one day the youth walked out and the black left town to start over. As an exit fee I tried to perform an act of re-covery. I became, even as I was writing the one book to my name, too old for that voice, and without a voice I can't tell any-one who I am or where I've been.

Francine Prose

She and I . . . and Someone Else

F irst there's the problem of our name, which would never have been a problem if she'd had another marketable skill and could have gotten a regular job. My revenge is that I watch her (and she knows that I am watching) smiling, a little rigidly, trying to be polite, telling herself that it's harmless, possibly even touching, the simple faith that anyone can come up with a funny new observation on the funny connection between her being named Prose and the only thing she knows how to do.

Anyway, she thinks they mean someone else. They are praising someone else's work or telling someone else that they borrowed her novels from the public library but unfortunately had to return them, unread, when the books were overdue. She thinks they mean another writer. But who? Surely not me. She thinks different people wrote each of her books, some more optimistic, inventive, funny, enraged, some more verbal and smarter than others, and all of them much wiser and larger spirited than she.

She is more shocked than I am by what turns up in her fiction. I know, as she does not, why lately she can hardly sit down to write without describing a hellish wedding or a vaguely sinister household pet.

I am not surprised, as she is, that variations on the same women and girls keep walking, uninvited, into her work. Who *would* invite these maladjusted semicatatonics to hover on the edge of life, always watching, watching, watching, with their eye for bad behavior and for what they're not supposed to see, and with the frightful vanity of their pathetic gift for being wounded by what wasn't meant to hurt anyone's feelings? I never know whether to believe her when she claims to have no idea why so many of her characters have extreme, complex, and voluble inner lives that they are incapable of expressing. *I* know why, because I've been watching her—that is, watching her watching. I want to tell her and her characters: Relax, girls! Lighten up!

Unlike her, I am not superstitious and do not suffer from bouts of existential dread or banal, demeaning worries about money or reputation. I am not distracted, as she always is, by any chance to travel, the promise of a good meal, or a phone call from her children's school: Someone's forgotten his clarinet!

Like her, I am paranoid and find myself believing that the most bizarre interpretation of events is the obvious explanation. For example: I often think that she would like me to disappear.

The evidence in support of this nearly incredible theory is that she never seems happier than when she is writing, when the work takes over, and the book (as she puts it, so unoriginally) seems to write itself. The characters are saying and doing things she hadn't planned at all. What pleases her is that she isn't there, she no longer feels herself present, and I . . .

Someone else is writing, and both she and I have vanished.

Henry Roth

The Interlocutor

Portrait of the Artist
as an old Fiasco

Roth

*H*e began to steal . . . in vindictive fury at first, after he rushed back from the hall at change of class, to find his fountain pen gone from the groove on the desk in which he had left it—only a minute before! His last and only fountain pen! Lousy bastards, sonofabitch bastard! He'd get even. He'd snitch someone else's pen. Frig him, whoever it was. . . . And what a cinch it turned out to be! Nothing to it. It was so easy *one,* he'd get another. Never have to worry about fountain pens anymore. Once you did it, had the nerve to do it, once was all that you needed to learn the knack.

He became a predator. . . .

Ira read the words of his first draft, the yellow typescript beside him: became! He could feel the grim sneer that bent his own lips: He became a predator from that day on. [And he had appended: "Indeed, it seems to me not in the matter of fountain pens alone, but as if their theft was symptomatic of the metamorphosis the entire psyche was already undergoing."]

—It had already undergone it.

Ah, yes, the point I was about to make, Ecclesias, and then forgot, as often happens to the writer, and probably more often to the aged one; so that the intended aside seems like a luxury, a self-indulgence. I wrote a novel, as you well know, Ecclesias, when I was young.

—Yes?

And the poor little nine-year-old tyke was victimized by the society around him, by forces in the environment around him, the good little nine-year-old tyke I might have written.

—Wasn't he?

Yes, of course. In the novel. But the reflection is a false one; it's quite distorted.

—Perhaps. But let me ask you: Why do you say that?

I say it because it is false to me, to the one I am, to the one I actually was. . . .

—At the time of writing?

At the time of writing, yes. That's exactly the point—I think of Joyce's Dedalus here, but that will have to wait. The writer imagined, given trifling variations of detail and time, that he was *faithfully* projecting, enacting, faithfully engrossing himself and his milieu, nay, faithfully representing himself in relation to his milieu. Do you follow me? The guy really believed he was purveying the truth, realizing actualities.

—Do you deny that he was victimized?

But not in that way! *He was part of the process.* And it is his part in the process he unconsciously suppressed, unconsciously omitted, and hence the picture is distorted. I can say the same thing another way: He was under the delusion that he was portraying truth, but in fact, he wasn't.

—How do you know he is now?

I don't—with any absolute certainty; only the relative certainty that I have at least taken into account, born witness to hitherto ignored relevancy.

—Could it be at the expense of art? Could it? . . . You are silent?

I don't know.

"Hey, Iry," Farley said in a subdued tone so that the other gym students wouldn't hear, "there's a guy up front in the next row, says that's his pen. It's yours, isn't it?"

"Sure it's mine," Ira blustered. "He's crazy!"

James Salter

We Two

O, I was fond of him in the early days, when only I knew him and everything he wrote was obvious or sentimental. He was more arrogant than promising but I saw beneath that. Over the years I did a great deal for him, helped him obliterate the past, the too familiar background, suggested things he should read or see. I think I gave him the idea of what he might be and also how to live close to that.

In the end I have aged faster than he has and his appearance is now different than mine—he is slimmer and more sure of himself. We are still mistaken for one another, however. Often there follows an expression of astonishment: they realize that I cannot be the one who wrote the book: "You're not like that at all." How can one reply to this, and it's probably true. Of course, occasionally no distinction between us is noted.

The fact is, I am like a caddie. I know everything about him and as much about the game. More, probably. I more or less advise him and tell him how to play, though he sometimes ignores it.

The bond which is unbreakable is that we have precisely the same interests, some of them concealed. In my case, at least, they are. There has been a long struggle—I have always urged him to express what he truly feels, but with only partial success. I wish he could be someone more like Larry Rivers, for instance, able to state things freely, but Rivers is a painter and works in a state of elation, or so it appears. Writing, at least as I judge it from knowing Salter, is different.

I sometimes like to imagine him, a more fortunate version of him, that is, in the 18th Century, the *ancien regime* with its enlightened discourse between fixed genders and classes, its dutiful maidservants and well-run houses based on upper and lower realms, old houses with fireplaces in their rooms and desks at which, beneath the scratching of a quill, line after line of direct and well-composed language appears. His actual methods are less serene. Lines crossed out, pages crumpled. His habits have become irregular and I have observed that he sometimes works best in a kind of vacuum that follows a late party or night of drinking, the world faded, his mind hugging the page. I have seen him sit motionless for long periods, waiting.

If I am now more distant from him, if in a way I doubt his reality and am little impressed by his bit of fame, there is still the curious question of actual possessions, which are mine and which his? The journals, of course, they will say are his but in truth I wrote them. And the books and carefully preserved, sometimes hidden letters and photographs? The letters—well, that's another thing—are they to me or him? Women occasionally write; they want to meet, for whatever reason, in New York or Paris. These letters are obviously meant for him; the writers do not even know me.

If in the end his writing has been about anything, I suppose it is about what it means to be a man, to live, behave, and die like one. He will be buried, perhaps, beneath a stone with carved letters that will soften and disappear in time though things inscribed on mere paper retain their brilliance. I know that this was his early ambition, that I be dust and he exist still.

Josef Škvorecký

Mitty and Me

I don't have a *doppelganger;* in my case it's simpler. Things either happen to me—and then I become a sort of Walter Mitty—or I get absorbed in the past—and Mitty enters his rickety time machine.

A few times I tried to drop Mitty and write the truth, the whole truth, and nothing but the truth. But Mitty is invincible.

The trouble is that I am a storyteller: I can only pass judgments on, and express the complexity of life through stories. But what does Mitty know about complexities?

One thing about him, though, is remarkable: The guy can write, and I have never been able to figure out how he does the trick. Since I am not a mystic, I don't believe in inspiration. I think it's just craftsmanship, and the title some people in my old country honor me with—Master—is of the category that includes master carpenters, chefs, or brewers.

But wait: Did Mitty go through those long years of apprenticeship, or was it me who did?

Perhaps, after all, I do have a *doppelganger.*

Jane Smiley

Borges, JCO, You, and Me

*W*ell, I don't believe them. I know who it is who says to my husband, "I'm going to work now," and turns away from him holding the baby, who is reaching out to me. I know whose hand turns the dingy brass knob of my office door, whose weight shifts to push the door open, who turns on the computer with a forefinger, whose impatience rises as the computer performs the same old ritual of getting started every day as if it has learned nothing. I know who it is who feels this seductive sliding feeling as the words appear on the screen, accumulating logical inertia. I know who it is because I feel the writing in my eyes and fingers and brain, more subtly, maybe, than the buildup of fatigue and lactic acid in muscles, but just as distinct. I am writing, I am reading what I write and writing more, while at the same time I am listening to the sounds of the baby in the next room, his vocal, though wordless, appreciation of the oatmeal my husband is feeding him. "Mmmm! Good boy," says my husband.

The real problem is *you*. You are developing some mistaken impression of me as you read this. You are consulting your own experience in order to discover how I am feeling, and your method, though the only one available to you, is all wrong for this. You used to not know me or think about me. Before you came along, all there was to my act of writing was that seductive sliding feeling followed by elation and the fatal wish to share it. I tried sharing with my mother, who made the mistake of offering suggestions; then I tried to share with boyfriends and lovers, who looked simultaneously perplexed and well-meaning. I shared with my writing classes, who were far too interested in their own work and not nearly interested enough in mine. I got an agent, but I suspected she had other favorites. I got an editor. We shared. She tried to convince me that we were sharing one hundred and ten percent, and I tried to believe her, but she kept offering suggestions. Through her efforts, I found you. I wish you well, but here is what I know about you from being myself a reader of other authors' work—everything you know about me is wrong, mostly because I have never been able to share with you the most important thing, which is that seductive sliding feeling.

Susan Sontag

Singleness

*W*ho's your favorite writer, a bumptious interviewer asked me many years ago. —Just one? —Uh-huh. —Then it's easy. Shakespeare, of course. —Oh, I would have never thought you'd say Shakespeare! —For heaven's sake, why? —Well, you've never written anything about Shakespeare.

Oh.

So I'm supposed to be what I write? No more? No less? But every writer knows this isn't so.

I write what I can: that is, what's given to me and what seems worth writing, by me. I care passionately about many things that don't get into my fiction and essays. They don't because what's in my head seems to me to lack originality (I never thought I had anything very interesting to say about Shakespeare), or because I haven't yet found the necessary inner freedom to write about them. My books aren't me—all of me. And in some ways I am less than them. The better ones are more intelligent, more talented, than I am . . . anyway, different. The "I" that writes is a transformation—a specializing and upgrading, according to certain literary goals and loyalties—of the "I" that lives. It feels true only in a trivial sense to say I make my books. What I really feel is that they are made, through me, by literature; and I'm their (literature's) servant.

The me through which the books make their way has other yearnings, too, other duties. For instance: as me, I believe in right action. But, as a writer, it's far more complicated. Literature is not about doing the right thing—though it is about expressiveness (language) at a noble level and wisdom (inclusiveness, empathy, truthfulness, moral seriousness). It's not about expressing me, either: I've never fancied the ideology of writing as self-expression.

And the books aren't me for an even deeper reason. My life has always felt like a becoming, and still does. But the books are finished. They liberate me to do, be, feel, aspire to something else—I'm a fierce learner. I've moved on. Sometimes I feel I'm in flight from the books, and the twaddle they generate. Sometimes the momentum is more pleasurable. I enjoy beginning again. The beginner's mind is best.

It's the beginner's mind I embrace, and permit myself, now—when I'm very far from being a beginning writer. When I began publishing thirty years ago, I entertained a simpler version of the figment that there were two people about: I and a writer of the same name. Admiration—no, veneration—for a host of books had brought me to my vocation, on my knees. So, naturally, I was scared . . . scared that I wasn't talented enough, worthy enough. I only found the courage to launch my frail vessel into literature's wide waters through a sense of two-ness that expressed, and enforced, my awareness of the gap between my own gifts and the standards I wished to honor in my work.

In fact, I never called what I did "my" work but "the" work. By extension, there was that one, the one who had dared to become a writer. And I, the one with the standards, who happily made sacrifices to keep her going, though I didn't think all that much of what she wrote.

Going on as a writer didn't allay this dissatisfaction, not for a very long time; it only upped the ante. (And I think I was right to be dissatisfied.) In my "Sontag and I" game, the disavowals were for real. Oppressed by as well as reluctantly proud of this widening mini-shelf of work signed by Susan Sontag, pained to distinguish myself (I was a seeker) from her (she had merely . . . found), I flinched at everything written about her, the praise as much as the pans. My one perennial form of self-flattery: I know better than anyone what she is about, and nobody is or could be as severe a judge of her work as I am myself.

Every writer—after a certain point, when one's labors have resulted in a body of work—experiences himself or herself as both Dr. Frankstein and the monster. For while harboring a secret sharer is probably not often the fantasy of a beginning writer, the conceit is bound to appeal to a writer who has gone on. And on. A persona now: enduring, and trying to ignore, the nibblings of alienation from the earlier work which time, and more work, are bound to worsen. It also playfully affirms the dismaying disparity between the inside (the ecstasy and arduousness of writing) and the outside (that congerie of misunderstandings and stereotypes that make up one's reputation or fame). I'm not that . . . image (in the minds of other people), it declares. And, with more poignancy: don't punish me for being what you call successful. I've got this onerous charge: this work-obsessed, ambitious writer who bears the same name as I do. I'm just me, accompanying, administering, tending to *that* one, so she can get some work done.

Then, more specifically, this doubling of the self puts a winsome sheen on the abandonment of self required to make literature that invariably incurs the stigma of selfishness in "real" life. To write, as Kafka said, you can never be alone enough. But the people you love tend not to appreciate your need to be solitary, to turn your back on them. You have to fend off the others to get your work done. And appease them—that issue is especially keen if the writer is a woman. Don't be mad, or jealous. I can't help it. You see, *she* writes.

Yeats said, one must choose between the life and the work.

No. And yes. One result of lavishing a good part of your one and only life on your books is that you come to feel that, as a person, you are faking it. I remember my merriment when, many years ago, I first came across Borges' elegy to himself, the most delicate account ever given of a writer's unease about the reconciling of life and work. Writers' pathos. Writers' humility. (I envied him the slyness of his humility.)

Rereading it now, I still grin. But I'm not so prone to make use of that balm to writers' self-consciousness which Borges' fable so charmingly evokes.

Far from needing the consolation of a certain ironic distance from myself (the earlier distance wasn't ironic at all), I've evolved slowly, with effort, in the opposite direction and finally come to feel that the writer is me: not my double, or familiar, or shadow playmate, or creation. (It's because I finally got to that point—it took almost thirty years—that I was finally able to write a book I really like: *The Volcano Lover.*) Now I think there's no escaping the burden of singleness. There's a difference between me and my books. But there's only one person here. That is scarier. Lonelier. And liberating.

Paul Theroux

Me and My Book

*W*hen I was small my family thought I was deaf. No, I was dreaming. Later on I heard of people harmed in accidents, scarred or crippled; and the same trauma produced in these victims mathematical genius, or an original line in art, or a quirk. *She hit her head on the dashboard and after that she couldn't stop eating.* I know that hunger.

Certain episodes in infancy or early childhood are a version of such accidents. In my case, I was left with a sense of separation. *He's not all there,* people said. The joke was true. I had been made lonely, and given a happy capacity to dream, and a need to invent. I did not understand the question, until I realized that my book was the answer.

People who have no idea who they are talking to have told me that they love Paul Theroux's book; yet I can see they aren't impressed with me. Of course! Other people have told me to my face that they dislike my book, but that I am a good sort. Why is that? As a person I am hurt and incomplete. My book is the rest of me. I inhabit every sentence I write! I tear them out of my heart!

After a long time in London I came to realize that I hated literary society for the very reasons I had once liked it: the shabby glamour, the talk, the drink, the companionship, the ambition, the business, and the belief: *You are your book.* I protested, *No, no—my book is better than me,* and went away.

Conspicuousness is not for me. My pleasure is that of a specter. I am calmest in remote places, haunting people who have no need of books and no idea what I do. I understand magicianship, murder, guilt, and motherhood; I also understand the demented people who late at night telephone strangers and whisper provocative words to them. Sometimes I feel like someone who has committed the perfect crime, an offender on the loose, who will never be caught. Please don't follow me, or ask me what went wrong. Please don't watch me eat.

My secret is safe. No one ever sees me write. One of the triumphs of a book is that it is created in the dark. It leaves my house in a plain wrapper, with no bloodstains. Unlike me, my book is whole and indestructible. In a reversal of the natural order, I am the shadow, my book is the substance. If my book is buried by time it can be dug up. The most powerful of the Chinese emperors, Qin Shi Huangdi—who tried—could not make printed books vanish.

I planned to be a medical doctor (who also wrote books) and on the days I cannot write, and especially when I am in a place like New Guinea or Malawi, I regret that I do not have a doctor's skill to heal. I am too old to learn now. But I would like to speak Spanish fluently, and tap-dance, and study celestial navigation. I intend to paddle for months down a long river, the Nile or one of the long Chinese rivers, or hike for a year or more across an interesting landscape. I dream of flying, using only my arms. I am well aware that some of these activities are metaphors for writing, but not the writing of my book.

Pretty soon I will be gone, and afterwards when people say, *He is his book,* the statement will be true.

Scott Turow

Young Him and Me

*M*y father was a doctor, an obstetrician. In our home, the phone was often shrilling suddenly in the still hours of the night, soon followed by the heavy sounds of my father's quick departure, routine disturbances that probably made me a fitful sleeper for life. Once I overheard my father tell a friend about the night before: Rushing from the house for the third time that week, he had caught sight of himself in a mirror. "You're up in the middle of the night," he told the ruined, haggard image he faced, "because some punk decided he wanted to be a doctor."

In my own looking glass, at the age of seventeen, I was sure I saw a novelist. I did not want my father's life of broken nights. Instead I thought that all the world's glory would reside in me if I saw my name on the spine of a book. Now I often find, somewhat in my father's fashion, that I would like a word or two with that young man—not to remonstrate or lecture, but to venture a few questions.

First of all, what was it that you thought you knew? What inchoate inner impulse was it you sought to follow? God knows, you were no Mozart. There were so many false starts, so many bad sentences and pages before you had even a faltering sense of the connection between all the teeming inner urges and words. Is it really possible then that you felt some glimmering intimation of the best moments in a writer's life—poised over the page, translating as the voices speak—or were you just on the road to all that imagined glory?

And what practical good did you think this writer would be to anybody else? Did you, child, consider your own children-to-be and what they might make of this Turow—he who pours their breakfast cereal distracted by the people speaking in his head, a heavy-footed fellow whose inspirations leave him treading through the night, troubling their sleep?

Did you think there was a realer you to be mined and brought forth? And have I now found him? Or did I misplace your future? Is this life, which seems so full to me, what *you* craved?

John Updike

Updike and I

I created Updike out of the sticks and mud of my Pennsylvania boyhood, so I can scarcely resent it when people, mistaking me for him, stop me on the street and ask me for his autograph. I am always surprised that I resemble him so closely that we can be confused. Meeting strangers, I must cope with an extra brightness in their faces, an expectancy that I will say something worthy of him; they do not realize that he works only in the medium of the written word, where other principles apply, and hours of time can be devoted to a moment's effect. Thrust into "real" time, he can scarcely function, and his awkward pleasantries and anxious stutter emerge through my lips. Myself, I am rather suave. I think fast, on my feet, and have no use for the qualificatory complexities and lame *double entendres* and pained exactations of language in which he is customarily mired. I move swiftly and rather blindly through life, spending the money he earns.

I early committed him to a search for significance, to philosophical issues that give direction and point to his verbal inventions, but am not myself aware of much point or meaning to things. Things *are*, rather unsayably, and when I force myself to peruse his elaborate scrims of words I wonder where he gets it all—not from *me,* I am sure. The distance between us is so great that the bad reviews he receives do not touch me, though I treasure his few prizes and mount them on the walls and shelves of my house, where they instantly yellow and tarnish. That he takes up so much of my time, answering his cloying mail and reading his incessant proofs, I resent. I feel that the fractional time of day he spends away from being Updike is what feeds and inspires him, and yet, perversely, he spends more and more time being Updike, that monster of whom my boyhood dreamed.

Each morning I awake from my present dreams, which as I age leave an ever more sour taste. Men once thought dreams to be messages from the gods, and then from something called the subconscious, as it seeks a salubrious rearrangement of the contents of the day past; but now it becomes hard to believe that they partake of any economy. Instead, a basic chaos seems expressed: A random play of electricity generates images of inexplicable specificity.

I brush my teeth, I dress and descend to the kitchen, where I eat and read the newspaper, which has been dreaming its own dreams in the night. Postponing the moment, savoring every small news item and vitamin pill and sip of unconcentrated orange juice, I at last return to the upstairs and face the rooms that Updike has filled with his books, his papers, his trophies, his projects. The abundant clutter stifles me, yet I am helpless to clear away much of it. It would be a blasphemy. He has become a sacred reality to me. I gaze at his worn wooden desk, his boxes of dull pencils, his blank-faced word processor, with a religious fear.

Suppose, some day, he fails to show up? I would attempt to do his work, but no one would be fooled.

Helen Vendler

The I of Writing

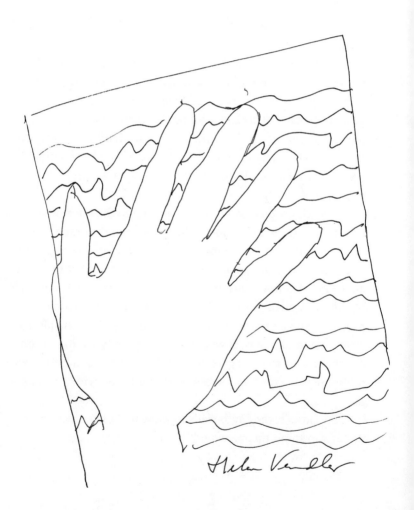

"*N*ot I, not I, but the wind that blows through me." I am deaf and blind writing; then suddenly I wake to the radio, and to ground covered with snow. Not asleep in body, not asleep in mind, but asleep in the senses and awake in an away, an otherness. The otherness is felt by my hand as it rewrites words— *the bronze decor, a shadow of a magnitude, so strength first found a way*. The hand is not female, the hand is not male; its *celestial stir* moves in a hyperspace neither here nor there, neither once nor now. The timeless hand moves in a place where memory cannot be remembered because it is part of a manifold undivided in time. The hand has no biography and no ideas; it traces a contour pliable under its touch. The braille of the words brushes my fingers and moves through them into my different calligraphy. The calligraphy tells less than the fingers feel; *sumptuous despair* loses its dark glamour as the hand falters after it. But the hand loves the contour, tracing obscure lineaments, translating them into language. Is the language signed? Only namelessly by its century and its country of origin, influencing invisibly the contour it has felt. The hand is anonymous, mine and not mine, even if my name signs what it has written.